Adaptive Project Planning

Adaptive Project Planning

Louise Worsley and Christopher Worsley

BEP BUSINESS EXPERT PRESS

Adaptive Project Planning

First published in 2019 by
Business Expert Press, LLC
222 East 46th Street, New York, NY 10017
www.businessexpertpress.com

ISBN-13: 978-1-94944-399-8 (paperback)
ISBN-13: 978-1-94999-100-0 (e-book)

Business Expert Press Portfolio and Project Management Collection

Collection ISSN: 2156-8189 (print)
Collection ISSN: 2156-8200 (electronic)

Cover and interior design by Exeter Premedia Services Private Ltd., Chennai, India

First edition: 2019

10 9 8 7 6 5 4 3 2 1

Printed in the United States of America.

Abstract

Projects are different. To be successful, they must meet the conditions defined by the project's stakeholders. Sometimes these conditions are explicit: it must be finished by this date, it cannot exceed this budget. Sometimes they are more subtle: the outputs, or the outcomes, must meet specific—often poorly articulated—criteria. The consequence is that the context, not the scope, of the project, is the real shaper of what has to be achieved, how it has to be done, and when. There is no pre-trodden path. To deal with this 'uniqueness' and the uncertainty it gives rise to, project managers have to plan.

Despite claims to the contrary, there is no single approach to planning a project, but for a given set of circumstances, there is a best one. This book takes you through many common planning situations you will meet. It uses stories of real projects to show how planning decisions alter depending on the project context. It discusses how resource-constrained planning differs from end-date schedule planning. It looks at what is different between cost-constrained plans and time boxing. It explores why you must plan when using Agile approaches, and how to plan for innovation.

Keywords

adaptive planning; Agile; project constraints; project management; project planning; resource modeling; scheduling; scope management

Contents

Preface

Appropriate planning of a project is the hallmark of a professional project manager—good planning is what sets apart great projects from accidents. It is what ensures that the executive actions undertaken remain connected to the goals and outcomes expected by the stakeholders. A project plan is a framework for decision making throughout the life of the project. It is hardly surprising then that the significance of planning in projects is much greater than in any other management discipline.

Today if you ask a project manager what the most important skill they require for their job is, they are likely to refer to areas such as stakeholder management, communications, leadership, or behavioral competencies. Is this because it is assumed that planning is obviously important and does not need to be mentioned or is it that project managers believe that with the right leadership style, communications and engagement they don't need planning? Do approaches such as Agile, which expound people over process, deliberately or inadvertently promote the obsolescence of planning?

After more than 70 years of experience in project management, and working with hundreds of professional, high-performance project managers, we know planning in projects is essential, but have also found the planning discipline to be both underused and misunderstood. Three factors we believe are responsible.

- *Planning is tricky to teach and to learn.* Methods and frameworks such as PMI and PRINCE2® discuss processes involved in planning, but neither gives real insights into what a good plan is and what proper planning feels like. The purpose of the planning process is to *structure* the controllable factors to make the project achievable within the set of success conditions (constraints and critical success factors).
- *Planning is confused with scheduling.* We do sometimes wonder if this is deliberate! We note the frequent and common

substituting of the one word for the other, and the way
sponsors accept Gantt charts when they ask for the project
plan. Microsoft Project may or may not be a useful scheduling
tool. What it most certainly is not, is a planning tool. What is
so saddening is that while every project benefits from having a
plan, it is less evident that all need a schedule, and many that
have one don't follow it.

- *Templates are introduced to standardize and simplify planning.*
  Possibly, in a well-intentioned effort to ease the learning curve
  for junior project managers and inexperienced sponsors,
  project management offices provide, promulgate, and sometimes mandate the use of a planning template. While without
  a doubt there is a single idea behind the need for a project
  plan, the impact of the differing contexts of projects frustrates
  the ambition for a single 'silver bullet' template.

In our research into what makes project managers successful, planning, along with monitoring and control, are the two areas where
high-performance project managers spend most of their time. What is
also clear from the findings is that the most distinctive characteristic is
their ability to use their experience and know-how to adapt their planning approach to meet the specific challenges of the project they were
managing.

There is no single approach to planning a project, but neither is project
planning a free-for-all. One consistent finding is that the context—
the environment within which planning takes place—determines the
approach that is most appropriate to use; which techniques and tools are
most suitable; and what factors to consider. The project-planning environment is itself a product of the set of constraints that bound the project,
and these constraints involve much more than time, cost and quality.
To plan effectively and appropriately project managers must take into
account both the source of the constraint and their relative significance or
priority—the hierarchy of constraints.

This book takes you through many of the common project planning
situations you will meet. It addresses how planning and planning decisions
alter depending on the constraint hierarchy: how resource-constrained

planning differs from end-date schedule planning, what is different between cost-constrained plans and time-boxing. It also discusses the challenges of integrating different product development life cycles, for example, Agile and waterfall, into a coherent and appropriate plan.

Using stories collected from over 70 years combined experience of running projects, teaching project managers, and developing project management capability in organizations, we have set out why planning is a core project discipline, how judgment affects the planning that is carried out, and what factors to take into account. In particular, we look to address these questions:

1. What strategic perspectives have to be maintained during planning.
2. What sequence of steps to use to develop the tactical aspects of a project plan.
3. How plans maintain the crucial link between the client's vision and the project's delivery.
4. How the planning sequence varies according to the conditions of success for the project, and in particular how the hierarchy of constraints affects the planning process.
5. How to determine the hierarchy of constraints in projects? And how and when to adapt your planning approach.

Acknowledgments

This book was made possible by the input and support of many colleagues and fellow project managers. Particular thanks are due to the patient reviewers and story providers who endured and provided feedback on our early endeavors: Ian Cribbes, Benedict Pinches, Linky van der Merwe, John Norman, and Ken Burrell. Without Prof. Tim Kloppenborg's encouragement, we would never have done it. Thank you to them all.

The stories shared in this book come from project managers all over the world. Some are anonymized because the source does not matter. Some, where knowing who was involved and why helps to understand the factors involved, are identifiable. Our thanks go to all those who have generously shared their experiences.

Writing this book caused us to revisit the many years of working with organizations and individuals to develop and deliver projects and programs—either directly—or like midwives, helping to bring new capabilities and new ambitions to life. To the people we have worked with, whether members of CITI, our project management company in the UK or PiCubed, its sister company in South Africa, or the hundreds of amazing clients, each of whom contributed to our understanding, and through that to the contents of this book, thank you.

After more than 25 years of both doing and teaching project management, and having been married to each other for 35 years, we are reasonably sure where our passion lies. As an MSc student once commented, "You guys have very different approaches when engaging with us, but together you make an unstoppable team." We hope you too find our combined thoughts on planning in project management both interesting and enjoyable.

CHAPTER 1

Planning a Project

Let's be clear. This book is about *project* planning. Planning is used in many other circumstances—operational management, strategy development, work packages, defect fixing, product development, and even personal to-dos, but projects are special management endeavors. Many techniques from general management are relevant and can be adapted readily enough, but there are differences. These differences can trap the unsuspecting, inexperienced project manager, who will often confuse the scheduling of task and activities with the planning of projects.

So, first things first, let's address these questions. What's a project? Why do you need to plan?

Planning to Manage Uncertainty

A project is a temporary organization set up to manage the inherent uncertainty caused when resources are assigned to undertake a unique and transient endeavor within a set of constraints and needs to integrate the outputs created into a changed future state that delivers beneficial outcomes.

Projects are often characterized as being unique, or at least 'relatively unique.' They may do what has been done before, but not by this team, or not in this way, and this means project managers must actively manage uncertainty. This is captured in our definition of a project, which is adapted from Turner (1999, 2003).

Project planning is the way we manage uncertainty. A plan is a view of the future, created from the state of knowledge at that time, and supported and extended by the inferences that experience and the underpinning models provide. As knowledge increases that view may change and a new route to the future must be captured by carrying out a re-plan.

A plan that documents exactly what everyone already knows really is a waste of everyone's time, no matter how beautifully written. It is the worst form of bureaucracy, with nothing new learned and nothing valuable achieved. A good plan makes clear what is uncertain and why, and what to do about it. What is known and what is not should be reflected in the very structure of the plan.

What is certain is why the project was set up. We also know what the stakeholders' regard as a good outcome. What is less certain is what the right tactics to adopt might be. These are uncertain because currently unknown events, events in the future, will influence them; whether it is by time passing, from the impact of risks, or higher than expected levels of productivity of a process.

Planning Connects Conditions of Success to Delivery

The other fundamental characteristic of projects we see reflected in the Turner definition is that projects are conducted within *a set of constraints* and create a *changed future state that delivers beneficial outcomes.*

The constraints and beneficial outcomes are an expression by the client and other stakeholders of the conditions of success for the project—and to plan successfully, you must know what counts as a success. Modern project management has replaced the earlier time, cost, and quality criteria with four conditions that have to be satisfied. Shenhar et al. (1997) set them out:

- Project efficiency
- Impact on the customer
- Direct business and organizational success
- Preparing for the future

The first factor neatly bundles up earlier ideas about traditional project management disciplines. The second and third reflect the realization that unless the project returns something of recognized value, its performance in terms of delivering outputs is worthless. The fourth focuses on what it is that the stakeholders have to bring to the party.

These new, tougher conditions for project success lead to the need for two key actions when planning a project. The first is to establish the 'mission' of the project—why it's being done, and what 'good looks like.' The other is how best to organize people, processes, and products to deliver that mission.

The Goal-Oriented Plan

If you are going on a journey, it's a good idea to know where you are going and how to recognize when you've got there. Might sound obvious, but many projects fail even that simple test. You really do need to know:

- *Purpose of the project*: the problem or opportunity it is addressing
- *Value of the project*: why is it worth doing—and to whom?
- *Objective*: what 'good looks like'—how to know the project has completed successfully
- *Scope*: what the project is expected to deliver in terms of physical things
- *Critical success factors (CSFs)*: what has to be in place for success
- *Risks*: what the main threats are to the success of the project

These are six distinct and different aspects of the project, and failure is much more likely if one or more of them is not known, or, which is more common, they are conflated and confused with each other. The usual culprit is a statement that purports to be an objective, but which is, in fact, a hotchpotch of scope statements, activities, benefits and other outcomes. Instead of a scalpel, the project manager has a club, with no way to adequately judge whether the project actions link to the project's purpose.

CITI's Project Mission Model™ (Figure 1.1) was developed to structure the way stakeholders, project managers, and project management offices go about this first part of planning.

The Project Mission Model™ explicitly distinguishes between the six perspectives. (Impacts and benefits are two ways of setting out the value, and count as one.) The combination of the views related one-to-another forms a holistic description of the project.

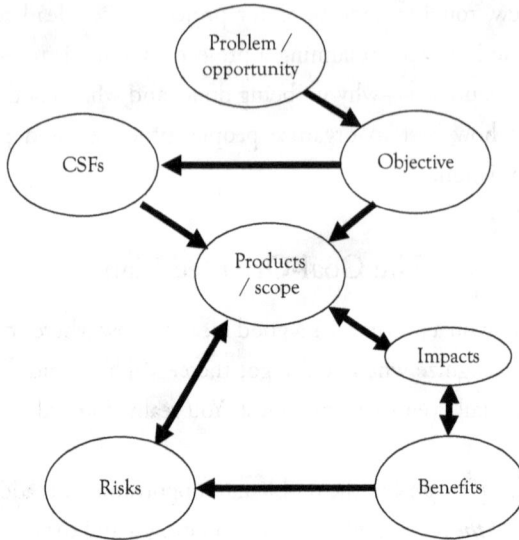

Figure 1.1 The project mission model™

As only key stakeholders can answer the first three questions, the early workshops should be run for these people. The project manager role is primarily an interested observer!

The Problem

Why is it being done? This first question is the proper starting point for any project. The answer should capture the purpose of the project.

The Benefits

Why is it worth doing? This is also a why question, and there is always a subtext to it, which is: To whom is it valuable? Benefits are measurable additions of value to the organization.

The Objective

What does success looks like? The response to this question should be a single statement describing the project's completion state, framed in terms of changed organizational (and possibly personal) capabilities. It should directly address the problem or opportunity.

The next three questions are the focus of workshops run later during project initiation with the project team and technical experts. Stakeholders are always welcome but rarely attend.

Products

What has to be produced? This is the central question for the project team. What is the project to build or buy to achieve the objective and cause the required impacts? At this level of planning, the focus is on the principal persistent products.

> *Persistent products or outputs:* Sometimes called deliverables, are what is left after the project is complete and which are instrumental in causing the outcomes (impacts and benefits) expected from the project.

It is worth noting that the objective is not the only source to consider when identifying products or outputs. In total, there are four sources, and together they establish the scope of the project. Inspection of Figure 1.1 shows four arrowheads pointing to the 'PRODUCTS' box.

In many projects, CSFs and the management of risk can generate a substantial number of additional products, as can the need to trigger required changes in behavior. Many of these outputs are temporary products but are still essential to the delivery of a successful project.

> *Temporary or non-persistent products*: exist in two forms:
>
> - Interim products necessarily created as part of the development process—such as designs, test rigs, test data, and so on—but do not form part of the delivered output.
> - Management products required when procedures do not provide evidence of progress or performance. Typical management products are project status reports, test results, and similar documents.

Risks

What could cause costs to rise or the value of benefits to fall? At this level of planning, the focus is on risks that should be exposed, shared, and agreed with the stakeholders. Risk analysis features as a continuing thread in all the planning. Even at this early stage, the risks identified should be listed in the project risk log.

> A risk is any potential event that could have a negative impact on achieving the objective or outcomes of a project, and, which you *intend to manage.*

Critical Success Factors

What has to be right? The third question is often the hardest to answer. As we will see, it has a profound influence on the conduct of the project and its planning. CSFs are usually derivative and can be identified by analysis of the assertions made in the objective and benefit statements. They are, however, ultimately determined and owned by the project stakeholders.

> *Critical success factors* are those things that must be present, and without which the project will fail. They are subject to special and continual management attention.

The Project Mission

The six views have been captured. What the world is to be like at the end of the project is understood, and why it is important to succeed, as well as what it is worth and to whom. In most cases, the basis for the solution is also agreed. All there is left to do is to ensure that the money and effort expended is structured, sequenced, and demonstrably connected back to the desired outcomes. So the next stage is to work out how to provide the outputs, what tasks to perform, by whom, and in what order.

Figure 1.2 shows an amended Project Mission Model™ that takes into account the factors needed to convert the strategic aspects of the

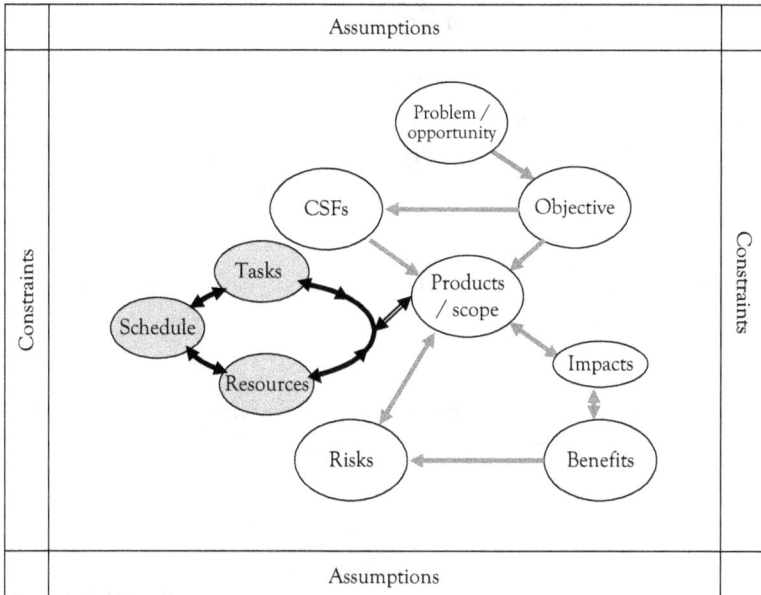

Figure 1.2 The full project mission model™

project into a tactical plan. There is a crucial link—a bridge—maintained between the outputs and structuring the project effort.

The bridge makes it possible for a plan to serve the stakeholder community of the project and the project team. If the link is broken project execution becomes detached from the purpose, and expectation management is blinded. What occurs over the bridge is the translation of what is wanted into how to get it.

You will have noticed the Project Mission Model™ is now framed by two fundamental planning elements. One is assumptions. Plans are very vulnerable to the set of assumptions made. When an assumption proves to be invalid, the project manager has to re-plan using different assumptions, and the stakeholders need to be made aware of what has happened.

Assumptions are those things held to be true for the purpose of project planning and management.

The other is constraints. We discuss these next as they play a pivotal role in the planning process, and will meet them again many times in this book.

The Role of Constraints and Critical Success Factors

CSFs set out what must be in place for the project to be a success by the stakeholders. The other conditions for success are identified by the project's constraints. Constraints feature in Turner's definition of a project quoted earlier, and in the PMI's definition, published in 2017:

> *A project is a planned set of inter related tasks to be executed over a fixed period and within certain cost and other limitations.* (PMI 2017)

A project constraint is *a condition that any solution must satisfy* and so defines what a successful solution looks like.

> A *constraint* is a boundary value which if breached means that the project plan is invalid and the project is working beyond its remit.
> A constraint is 'owned' by someone other than the project manager.

Seven frequently encountered constraints (and CSFs) are listed as follows. There are, of course, others.

Temporal: some projects must be completed by an end-date determined externally and cannot be changed. Typical examples are the legislative programs for financial regulation such as Basel III (2011) and Kings III (2009).

Budget: these projects are limited explicitly by a capped fund. Projects funded by granting bodies are usually cost-constrained in this way.

Resources: a close cousin to budget constraint, but the impact and planning response is markedly different in these projects. Very often, the problem is to do with not having access to a scarce and non-replaceable resource; for example, world-class research scientists.

Mission-critical: when what a project delivers must meet specific 'no-fail' criteria. Examples of this type of project are: NASA staffed launches, nuclear industry projects, and irreversible business process changes.

Stakeholder-intensive: when the success of a project is determined by inviolable, non-negotiable acceptance criteria (ACs) set by the stakeholders. Examples of such projects are the Scottish Parliament building and the Integrated Rapid Transit program in Cape Town.

Innovation/research: the success of these projects is dependent on the delivery of outputs that trigger outcomes that are not explicitly anticipated—including the identification of 'blind alleys.' The story of the accidental invention of 'post-it notes' and Viagra are both well-known examples. Many modern research projects adopt this approach.

Operational: these projects can only succeed if the operational performance of an ongoing enterprise continues without disruption. This constraint often requires highly responsive planning. Classic examples are enhancements to products and processes used in hospital and financial systems.

The Delivery Plan

The project mission is agreed. It may change under the pressure of technical infeasibility, but the pre-requisites for planning *how* to deliver are now in place. So what's next to do? Is there a process? How do you go about structuring people, processes, and products to deliver the mission? Well, there is a process. It has seven steps, and as you will see in the later chapters the sequence varies to reflect the hierarchy of the constraints, but the steps are the same. The standard sequence of steps is easy to remember. It is 'C' followed by an alphabetic stammer:

C-Constraints
P-Products (outputs)
P-Processes (tasks)
R-Resources
R-Risks
S-Schedule
S-Stakeholders

Steps from Constraints to Resources

Once you have determined the constraints, the steps to completing the project plan are:

First, determine the…

Products—the outputs you need to achieve the outcomes: *Then look at the…*

Processes—tasks that will get you these products: *This will suggest the types of…*

Resources—capabilities needed for the tasks: *These three aspects each can create…*

Risks—that threaten the achievement of the objective: *These four integrate into a…*

Schedule—activities with resources sequenced: *And all together must meet…*

Stakeholder—expectations: It is their view that determines whether a plan is acceptable.

There is a temptation to see planning as being a top-down process, done in a single pass. This is most decidedly not the case! As Figure 1.3 shows, each step can cause you to go back, to revisit choices and decisions made higher up the chain. The two immovable things—the only two things project managers cannot change—are the constraints and the objective. They have to get permission from the sponsor and other key stakeholders

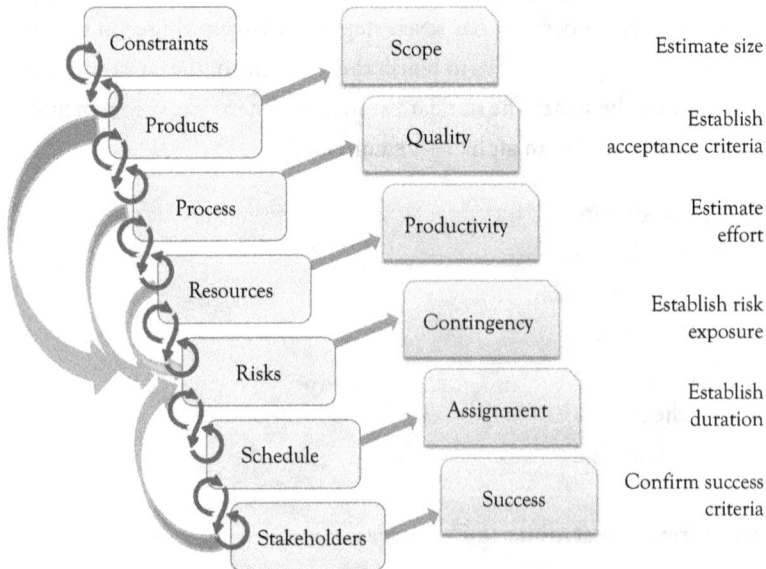

Figure 1.3 The basic planning steps and their associated knowledge areas

to change either of those otherwise they are in genuine danger of damaging that crucial link, the bridge, between the Project Mission Model™ and the executable plan.

Step one establishes the 'box' in which the plan has validity—what are the constraints the project, and hence the plan, must work within. Which constraint is the most important may not immediately be apparent. Sponsors and stakeholders are not always clear in their own minds as to what is truly important. However, there is always a hierarchy. Sometimes the only way to establish what the real constraints are is by engaging with the stakeholders during planning, by posing situations and seeing how issues are resolved.

The next step involves elaborating on the outputs or products. You should avoid identifying the processes at this stage. Projects are a vehicle for producing products—or outputs. Discussing tasks before knowing what the outputs are is usually a grievous error. So list the outputs! Once you have a list of the set of products, you will have definitively established the scope of the project—an excellent basis for planning.

Start by agreeing what the principal persistent products (those outputs that will remain after the project has closed) should be. This will be, for the most part, what the project must deliver to meet its objectives. This list can be developed as a product breakdown structure (PBS), see Figure 1.4.

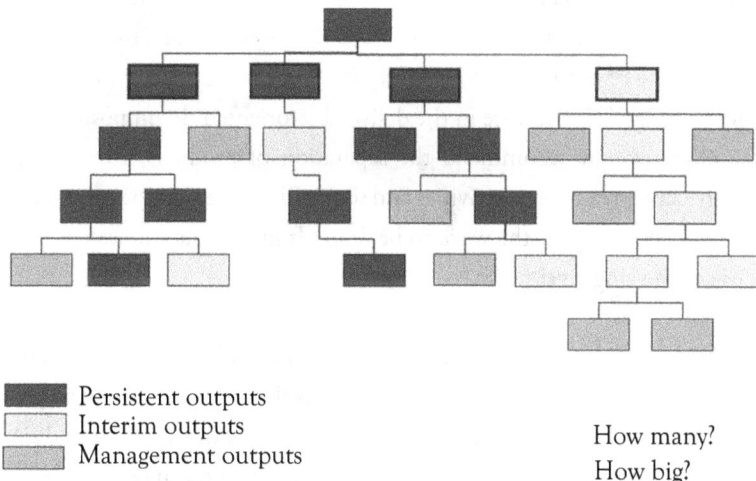

Persistent outputs
Interim outputs
Management outputs

How many?
How big?

Figure 1.4 A product breakdown structure (PBS)

Once you've set out the outputs, and this may involve several iterations, it is now appropriate to define the tasks (methods, techniques, and tools) to acquire (create or purchase) each product. As you are doing so, it is also valuable to establish the level of quality—the acceptance criteria (ACs)—that the stakeholders expect. The ACs are usually negotiable, unlike constraints and CSFs. By establishing the ACs now, the likely processes to be used can be determined as well as the likelihood and type of defects to expect.

The task list, which can be organized into a logical work breakdown structure (WBS), is not yet sequenced. Best practice is to keep the PBS and the WBS as distinct elements, as is strongly encouraged by PRINCE2®. However, many methods and the PMI allow or even promote both products and tasks to be defined in a single structure, confusingly called a WBS.

The PMBOK (2013) uses the term WBS, standing for work breakdown structure, instead of PBS. Our view is that this was an early PMI misnomer, which once made they felt unable to correct. The definitions of the WBS entries, that they must be nouns; that each element is a deliverable are worthy, but even their own examples include ambiguities. Saying a deliverable is a 'door painted' is just a way of sneaking in an activity! We suspect the deliverable is a 'door' with associated acceptance criteria such as the color should be appropriate; it should be weatherproof, and so on. To confuse things even more, the 6th edition of the PMBOK (2018) now explicitly encourages 'work to be performed' entries to feature in the deliverable-oriented decomposition.

We strongly recommend the separation of products from tasks, deliverables from work activities and so use PBS to set out the products, and WBS to lay out the work to be done. It just seems a more natural use of the language!

Once the WBS is created, estimates of skill and likely resource demand can be made. These, too, should reflect the level of uncertainty and be provided as ranged estimates. The effort is derivative of the numbers and size of each product set out in the PBS. The effort demand can be modeled in yet another breakdown structure—one that reflects the resource structure of the organization—an OBS. The choice of process inevitably dictates the kind of resource you need—the skill sets necessary to carry out the process.

Steps from Risks to Stakeholders

So, we have now considered 'CPPR'—the constraints, products, processes, and resources. The next 'R' is the set of risks. As you step through the planning sequence you will identify risks: risks from the products (level of performance), risks from the processes chosen (types of defects arising), and risks from the resources (capability and productivity) you are going to use.

Now, and only now, are you in a position to devise the schedule—the sequence with which your project is going to order the tasks and activities, and when to engage the various resources. Without a doubt, the appropriate scheduling of effort time within calendar time is what distinguishes good project managers from less capable ones—it is a fundamental skill. It is also, however, secondary to and derivative of the planning process.

Typically, schedules are based on the WBS, and it is good practice to create work packages—sets of tasks with their resources—for each primary deliverable. With this approach, it is vital that dates in those sub-schedules are coordinated with the master schedule, and that the master schedule is correlated with the business milestones within the overall project plan.

So there you have it. All the technical aspects of planning set out in a step-by-step process. However, we are not yet finished! There is one more 'S' to factor into the plan—and it can be a game-changer.

This last 'S' is the stakeholders. The crucial test the plan must survive is whether the various solutions, trade-offs and tactical considerations made, meet the stakeholders' needs and expectations. If it does, you have a viable plan; if it does not, it will have to be changed.

This final point has an enormous impact on the approach to planning. The plan is not yours. It is not primarily for the project manager, it is for the stakeholders, and in particular for the needs of those stakeholders that form the governance group for the project. This has all sorts of consequences, from determining the plan's contents, the appropriate format, to the level of detail it should go to, and the communication needs it has to address.

So, that's nearly it for planning many straightforward projects. There is just one more topic to discuss. How does the hierarchy of constraints affect the planning process?

Hierarchy of Constraints

Though project managers are often presented with a set of constraints that they are informed they must meet, it turns out that, within a given project, some constraints are more important than others. This difference in ranking is one of the most important factors when deciding how to plan. Table 1.1 illustrates four common hierarchies of constraints found in projects.

When the type of constraint at the top of the hierarchy is different, the plans—and the planning tools to be used—differ. Plans drawn up under one hierarchy are not readily interchangeable with one drawn up under a different one.

In the following chapters we explore stories and insights for each of the seven frequently encountered constraints (and CSFs):

- Temporal
- Budget
- Resources
- Mission-critical
- Stakeholder-intensive
- Innovation/research
- Operational

Table 1.1 Different hierarchies of constraints

Enhancement to product	New financial product	Prestigious HQ	Space shuttle
Budget	Legal compliance	Stakeholder	Safety
Deadline	Deadline	Quality	Quality
Quality	Quality	Process	Process
Process	Budget	Deadline	Budget
	Process		

There are, of course, others! And that matters because the reality is that project characteristics on complex projects do change during the project. A project may initially be driven by a hard deadline, but then issues arise that can only be resolved by acquiring scarce resources and the characteristics of the project change fundamentally, and a re-plan is forced.

During the 1980s, we were involved in research into what makes project managers successful. You can read more about this in *The Lost Art of Planning Projects* (Worsley and Worsley 2019). What seems to be the distinguishing characteristics of high performing project managers is that they are excellent project diagnosticians, and they have an extensive toolkit to pull upon when deciding what combination of approaches will be right for any particular project. They understand the impact on the hierarchy of constraints on their projects and adapt appropriately to the different challenges they present.

We hope the insights from these different project types inspire reflections on how you should approach your project planning. At the end of each chapter, we reflect on what's been discussed and pose questions for you to consider in light of your own experiences, your projects, and what makes them different. Do take time to give these some thought or better still discuss with project colleagues back in your organization.

Reflections

This chapter introduces two fundamental models: one to establish the strategic aspects of a project plan—the project mission—the second, the tactical concerns. It also set outs a structure for a plan that reflects the different levels of volatility.

Consider for your projects and from your own experiences:

1. How do you go about developing a plan? Is there a process you can share with others? Do you use a template to guide you? What advantages does that give? Are there any disadvantages?
2. How do you record time-dependent information used in planning, such as issues, risks, and decisions?
3. When sponsors ask for the status of the project, what are they asking for, and what do you give them?

4. How frequently do you review your plan? Your logs? Your schedule? Do you and project team members use the schedule to direct what they do on a day-to-day basis?

5. During development, do you discuss your plans, with the project office? The sponsor? The stakeholders? Colleague project managers? Your team? What aspects do you share, and why?

CHAPTER 2

Schedule-Driven Planning

In 1988, in San Diego California, a competition was conducted to build a house from the ground up in four hours or less. The competing groups could not use pre-fabricated parts, they had to put in the foundations, and they had to abide by all of the strict Californian building codes, including being earthquake resistant! Oh, and they also had to paint it, furnish it, install the kitchen, and create a garden with shrubs and a lawn. They took just two hours 45 minutes.

To achieve this remarkable feat the project demanded the coordination of some 370 contractors; including landscape gardeners, roofers, plasterers, plumbers, and electricians. All of the professions that would typically be involved in a building of house but would not usually work together at the same time!

The planning demanded extreme measures to ensure that there was no rework, and no unnecessary activity: the roof had to fit the walls—the first time; the plumbing was in before the floor went down, and the dry-skin walls were up before painting commenced. None of the items on the list is unusual in building a house, but in this case, because of the extreme time constraint, the processes used to deliver them were.

You can see highlights of the four-hour house on YouTube. Scan this QR code (Figure 2.1) with your smartphone, or enter the URL into your

https://youtu.be/oDB1O5cadQw

Figure 2.1 QR code for the four-hour house and a short URL

browser. Perhaps you might take a break to have a look at the clip and consider the question: What did the project planners use to trigger the deployment of such innovative processes by such traditional building practitioners?

Compressing Time Means More Planning

You will have realized by now that this was no four-hour house! That was merely the time it took for the implementation stage. As the video explains, the design and planning taken together—and they *have* to be taken together as we will see—took over six months. The detailed planning, re-planning, scheduling, and the testing of the schedule was at least as time-consuming as the technical design. So the project took more than six months. Planning under extreme constraints takes time!

One extraordinary achievement made possible by this project planning was that despite the extreme workforce build-up index (MBI), it used virtually the same total resource as under normal conditions. Figure 2.2 illustrates the differences between the MBI for a standard house build and the four-hour house.

In Curve 2, we can see the long pre-execution build-up where a relatively small group is involved in designing, planning and coordinating the scheduling process. Then within the space of a few minutes, the number of resources escalates rapidly from a few to over 370 people on site.

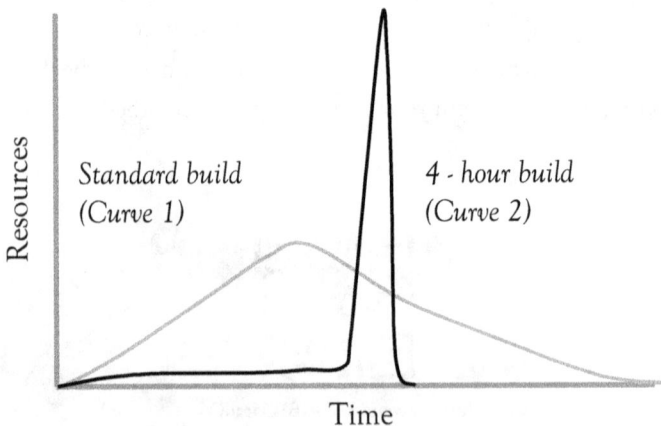

Figure 2.2 Comparing workforce build-up indices (MBIs)

370 people working for three hours is just over a thousand person-hours, which is approximately the same level of effort to build a house normally, over a seven to 10 week period. However, what any PMP qualified project manager will know, typically when you crash a schedule by adding more resources, individual productivity declines steeply. How did they manage to avoid this in this project?

Well, it didn't happen by accident! In time-constrained projects, the planning is intensive. Alternate routes (schedules) are set out to deal with unexpected and unwelcome events, and the level of task and productivity monitoring is exceptionally high. (In the video, there is a glimpse of monitors with walkie-talkies allowing the project manager to coordinate across the activities.) In such a project, shortcuts do lead to long delays. Unresolved issues and risk events, without associated pre-defined management actions, kill schedules. The impulse to start quickly and "get on with it," so often asked for by sponsors and key stakeholders needs to be resisted.

Another aspect to note in this project was that the schedule was set up to achieve completion within four hours, but on the day, it was finished in less than three hours. The schedule had been designed to take advantage of tasks completing early. Allowing for this is a strong argument for keeping high fan-out and high fan-in nodes out of the task sequence, and shows why and how allocating contingencies at the activity level is such a good idea.

Fan-outs occur when one task triggers the initiation of several others. Fan-ins are when, to complete one task, many others need to finish. Both of these are often accidentally created by careless scheduling practices. When running a project assurance exercise and the project has used PERT or a similar scheduling tool, it is an easy visual check—you see structures like those shown in Figure 2.3.

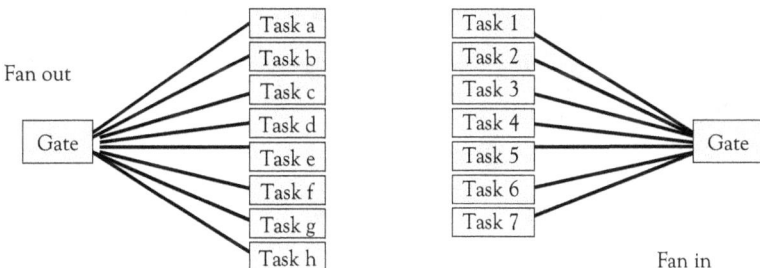

Figure 2.3 Risks created by scheduling

Knowing how to plan and schedule for 'as soon as possible' (ASAP) and taking opportunities that present themselves to accelerate a schedule is not straightforward using standard PERT charting. If you model using aggressive activity duration estimates, the likelihood of slippage is high, and the schedule quickly becomes out-of-date. If you model with built-in contingency—a more normal practice—it tends to hide the target duration and to create 'wait' states, not something you want when looking for opportunities to go faster. And if you create lots of dummy activities to model the contingency explicitly, the reporting process becomes overly complicated, as does the representation of the schedule. Figure 2.4 illustrates the problem with using aggressive durations versus tasks with the contingency 'hidden' in the duration number in classic PERT charts.

A possible alternative to PERT and its critical path approach, in this type of scheduling environment, is to adopt the critical chain approach to scheduling a project developed by Goldratt (1997). Figure 2.5 shows, for comparison, the way a critical chain approach models the same problem. It also shows how it deals with contingency and access to critical resources through the use of buffers. The critical chain schedule shows a time-constrained project with seven activities and a total aggressive activity duration estimate of 11 days. The end-date is set by adding the project buffer

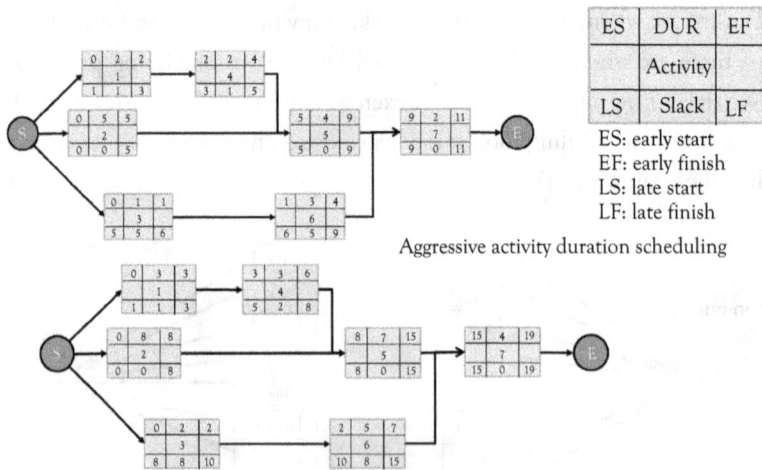

Figure 2.4 **Scheduling for opportunities**

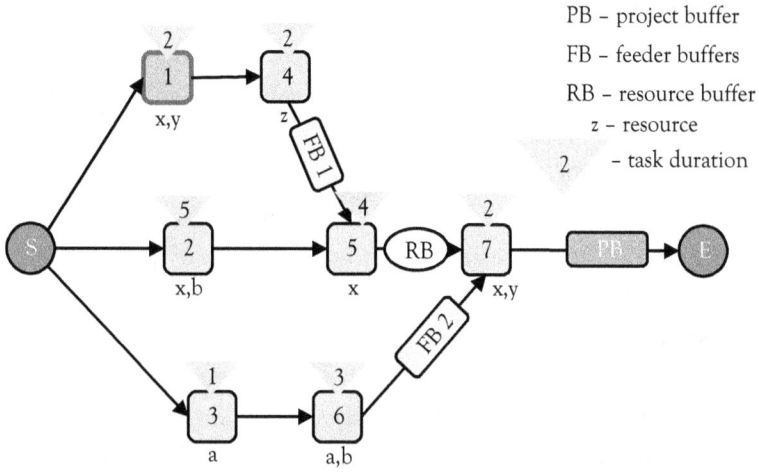

PB – project buffer
FB – feeder buffers
RB – resource buffer
z – resource
2 – task duration

A critical chain schedule

- Project buffer: a buffer to protect project end-date
- Feeding buffer: buffers to protect the critical chain
- Resource buffer: buffers to assure the availability of resources

Figure 2.5 Using critical chain sequencing

to the aggressive duration estimates. To protect the critical chain are two feeder buffers; to protect the end-date there is a project buffer; and to ensure tasks are not held up for lack of availability of a necessary resource, there is a resource buffer.

When Time Is of the Essence

What are the causes of elapsed-time delays in the projects with which you and I get involved? Waiting for approvals and authorization to proceed are common culprits. When building a regular house, the need to wait for building inspectors to visit the site and provide approval documentation interrupts workflow. To address this, in the four-hour house project, the building inspectors were on-site during the build, and their activities planned into the tightly scheduled process, thus eliminating the usual build-wait-build cycle.

In the UK, a large retail group suffered a catastrophic fire, which destroyed one of its primary distribution centers. Although insurance would cover the loss of stock, the business could fail due to the disruptions to its logistical and supply chains. A rebuilt distribution center was needed quickly if a corporate crisis was to be averted.

The Board agreed to allocate a single sponsor, who would take responsibility for the decision making during the build. One of the first deliverables was a luxuriously appointed temporary accommodation onsite for this sponsor. He lived and worked there for the duration of the project. There was never a delay when issues arose. The project manager simply walked the sponsor to the problem and waited for the answer—the governance process had been integrated into the project. The new site was delivered and made operational in record time. As the project manager reported, "Having the sponsor onsite was more important than any other factor in bringing this project in so quickly."

As every experienced project manager knows, often the real enemy is calendar time. You can manage effort time, but not the passing of hours. The trick we all have to learn is how to package effort to maximum advantage. When the challenge is to maintain high levels of productivity, the project manager has to consider all of the things that would, in normal circumstances, result in increasing the elapsed time:

- Resources (people, supplies, and tools) not on-hand when they are needed
- Resources not competent or unsure of how best to do something
- Roles and responsibilities unclear—who does what and when
- Delays caused by poor communications between individuals and teams
- Non-collaborative behaviors between individuals and teams
- Unresolved issues

It is for these reasons that planning is not an activity for a master planner working on their own. Planning involves active consultation with teams and their leaders. They know best the needs and in what sequence to start activities; and what can be allowed to run in parallel safely. Engaging with subject matter experts (SMEs) is a crucial part of gaining insight and commitment.

Constructive Use of Constraints

A slight modification of the CPPRRSS planning process allows for a very rapid iteration between the products (outputs) and possible processes, thus providing the opportunity for innovation when that would be advantageous.

Consider the case of laying the foundations in the four-hour house. The *project management* question is not "How do we lay the foundation?" It is, "How can we walk on a foundation—that meets all of the acceptance criteria—in 45 minutes?" The process of installing a ceiling is known, the question given to the SME is "How do we ensure it is in place and the room ready for the next activity in 12 minutes?"

The way the solutions affect the scoping, costing, and scheduling, not the technical engineering aspect, is what fully engages the project manager during the planning. Initially, standard processes are chosen because they have the lowest technical risk. In the context of projects that means that the defects they create (all processes generate defects) are known, as are the workarounds. People know how to recognize them and where to look for them.

If, however, the standard processes are too slow or create unacceptable dependencies with other activities, this makes them unusable; they threaten the success of the project. Under these circumstances, innovative approaches, together with the increased monitoring and control they demand, are indicated. Better by far to take a managed risk than to plan to fail. This is the role constraints have in project management. They validate the plan. They are not, therefore, as Goldratt and Cox's (1984) operational view would have it, obstacles or hindrances to the achieving of the objective, but shapers and guides to the best options to take.

Often, when seeing the four-hour house for the first time, project managers grumble—"Yes but ..." and will point to special circumstances:

strong stakeholder backing, skilled and motivated people, publicity. Some points they make are factually accurate, others mere surmise, but all are in the power of a project manager to make a reality for themselves.

One observation sometimes made is that the project was "allowed" to build a test house first. It's almost as if it was cheating or unfair to rehearse the tasks, the schedule, and the innovative practices to identify problems and areas where productivity could be improved before the final build. As we will see in Chapter 5 on mission-critical projects, it's not unfair; it's fundamental!

Another, sometimes overlooked, part of the planning was running the project party before the start of the project; a sensible and project-like thing to do. Projects, in general, are characterized by having transient teams, groups of people who have not worked together or even know each other, and who, after the project, will go their separate ways. So, why project managers run after-project parties is a bit of a mystery to us; while holding a party at the beginning to establish and encourage team relationships seems like money well spent.

Personal discipline is needed when adhering to a schedule, but not at the expense of an appropriate level of 'can-do' attitude. In the four-hour house, the rehearsing activities and the creation of good, rapid communication links between teams were emphasized. Each team had a clear view of what their role was regarding both the outputs and the outcomes they needed to deliver. They were also acutely aware of the interdependencies with other groups. These were made explicitly visible in the planning.

Roles and responsibilities by the team and by individuals were set out in the plan. The schedule, when *it* was drawn up, was a series of minutely detailed and timed steps. The difference being that the scheduled activities were set out by the SMEs, not the project planner.

Why? Because when a project member is unclear or hesitant about how and when to act, delays occur in project execution. De-complexifying the 'who does what' is part of the project planning process. In a complex project, clarity will come in and out of focus over the life of the project as activities change and new people become involved with the project. The project manager has to monitor the 'team state of understanding,' restructure roles, and re-communicate as many times as necessary. This is different from telling a person how to do their job—they know that better than you do.

This brings us to the importance of communication.

The Importance of Communication

"We are ready for you."; "Approvals have been completed."; "We need more paper."; "It's gone wrong!";" Wait, we are not ready."; "What should I do now?" are typical communications between individuals and teams that need to be swiftly and unambiguously transmitted to maintain productivity. That means establishing controlled and effective communications within the execution process.

In the four-hour house, monitors with walkie-talkies (a 1980s equivalent of mobile phones and messaging systems) were dedicated to the task of communication between teams and between teams and the project manager. Today we have many modes of communication from which to choose. The concern remains the same, however: How to ensure that the communications remain coherent and coordinated? The project plan should inform and facilitate appropriate targeting of communications, Who needs to know what, and when? are the fundamental questions. Shotgun communication, spraying everyone with everything, is a direct route to project failure!

"The teams are working together so well. Normally they would be throwing hammers at each other!" commented a senior building inspector involved in the four-hour house. Many projects are set up to work within functional boundaries and for a good reason. Functional groups generally work best within their own function. Many of the most valuable projects, however, involve cross-functional transient team structures, with groups having to find ways of working together, crossing existing functional and cultural team boundaries. Work, which requires acting outside these boundaries, is more difficult to achieve. So, are there any good ways?

In the four-hour house, perhaps the critical contributor to the successful cross-team work was the competition itself. This unusual situation created the motivation for teams to act in the best interests of the project rather than focus on narrow functional agendas. The collaborative involvement in the planning provided broader visibility and transparency on what was to be achieved. The planning process essentially gave the teams 'permission' to look over the fence and seek out approaches to optimizing productivity in how they engaged with other teams.

This situation can be simulated in more everyday projects, and in time-constrained projects, it may well be worth the effort. In a post-merger project in which the end-date was immovable, and there were seven teams from different functions collaborating, two objects were swapped between the teams. One was a plaster cast of a hot potato. This was given to the team that was causing delay. No team wanted it and tried hard to get rid of it as quickly as possible. The second was a small anvil with two acorns on it. This was given to the team that was working on time-critical activities and was a sign they should not be interrupted without a serious reason. The results were extraordinary! Motivation levels were high, communication within and especially between the groups was excellent, and the outcome was an impressively performing on-time project.

This need to find ways of engaging with other teams in supportive ways was captured well in an interview with a portfolio manager in a leading South African-based grocery retailer. She explained some of the benefits that they were getting from using techniques such as Kanban and Jira.

> We are not a full-blown Agile environment," she said, "But we've found that techniques such as work-in-progress, job-cards and streams have been a very effective way of building energy, commitment, and collaboration between technical teams, and invites much closer business ownership.

They had found that by sharing and making visible the 'to-dos,' issues, and challenges, the contributing teams found more collaborative solutions. The teams could see the problems and then work together to find answers, which they would not have found on their own.

Protecting the End-Date

In any project, even one as meticulously planned as the four-hour house, problems will arise to which the project will have to react quickly. Many can be anticipated and management actions formulated on what might be done should the situation arise. This is the basis of sound risk management—the identification of possible events and forethought around actions to be taken to reduce or deal with any negative impacts should they arise.

For the four-hour house, the possibility of rain was a real concern. Of course, rain of itself is not a risk—it's just something that could happen. The actual risk, appropriately stated, is that if it should rain, the timing of various processes will be extended (the consequence or impact of rain falling). Given the time constraints within which the project is operating, this is a genuine threat. In a time-constrained project, the first consideration must be how events and their consequences may affect the end-date.

You can see how the constraint simplifies the identification of appropriate risk strategies and management actions. You can't avoid rain, and you can't transfer the risk. You can reduce the likelihood of it raining by choosing the time of year and picking a 'window' of predicted good weather, but for the rest, it means protecting yourself against the worst of the delays caused by wetting. It should also be clear that 'fix-on-failure' or mitigation is not an option. So, it means spending money ahead of the possible event. (See Figure 2.6.)

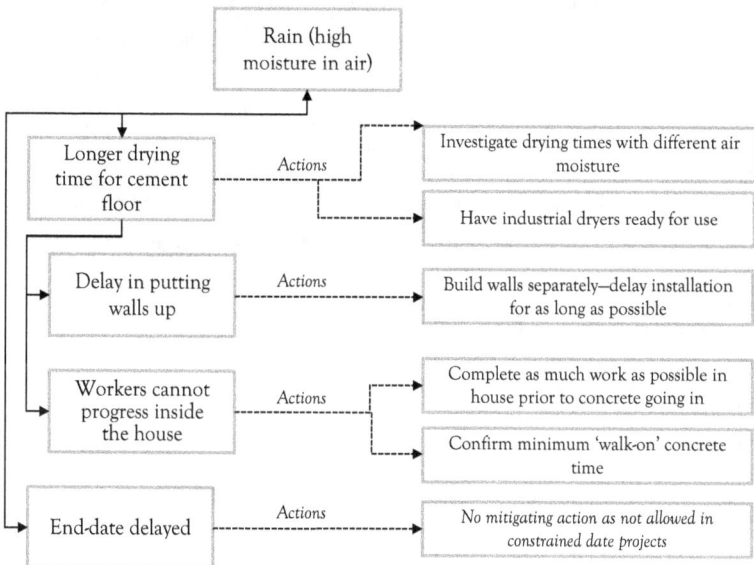

Figure 2.6 Risk management actions options tree

Breaking Process Norms

Several years ago, we were working on a severely time-constrained project, which involved the demutualization of a major insurance company in the UK. Legislation demanded that the company ensured its name always correctly reflected its legal status. To ensure compliance, and to avoid expensive legal issues, before demutualization the company had to use its old name, and after demutualization, all public documentation had to use the new name. This program, with a legally determined fixed end-date, was made more complicated by the fact that the actual demutualization date had to be kept secret from all but the inner circle of managers to guard against insider dealing.

One of the projects in the program was set up to ensure all documentation and external references (websites, and so on) would be ready to be moved to the new company name on the required date—called D-Day. The first problem was precisely how many such documents were there? Acknowledging that it was possible that some might be missed, the sponsor demanded that no outbound document could leave the building on, or for 10 days after D-Day without authorization from one of six people. To give you a feel for the size of the problem, by D-Day minus 10, about 5,000 legally binding outbound documents had been identified, with perhaps six times that number of internal documents. All of them had been or had to be altered.

How to make all these changes and meet the strict deadline? The process in place for all legally binding documents was that any change had to be approved, and in many cases to be carried out, by the compliance team. At that time, the company's actuarial team always carried out compliance.

Initially, they were actively involved in the planning process, and their estimate for completing the checks was in the order of three calendar years. An answer that paid tribute to the thoroughness of their procedures, and their incomprehension of the needs of the business! Even finding more of these very scarce resources—a pretty long shot—would make little difference to meeting the hard deadline. An impasse resulted with the compliance team insisting this was the way it had to be done, and the project rejecting their estimates as unacceptable.

The most senior of the stakeholders got involved. The project team planners and the compliance teams were brought together and the reality of the hard constraints—the legal deadline—was used to force a shared exploration of how to solve the problem. For this project, it was finally agreed that the 'normal' process just could not be used. Working as a task force, the actuaries and the project members worked to solve the problem: How do we deliver sufficiently 'safe' legally binding words in 5,000 documents in seven elapsed months? Once the problem had been set out in the right terms, the players found the solution.

In the four-hour house, one of the most extended elapsed time activities was the concreting of the foundations and floor. Concrete, mixed and laid conventionally, typically takes three to four days to dry before it can be built on safely, which the teams just didn't have. During the planning stages, various solutions were considered, and in the end, the chosen process involved chemically heating the concrete. This hot concrete could be poured and would be walkable on within 20 minutes. More expensive, a higher risk than the normal process, but a process that would meet the primary constraint for their project—being quick!

In time-constrained projects, operational processes, resourcing solutions, and their associated risks, which are the standard ways to do things, may have to be modified to deliver the project outcomes. Innovation and creativity must be encouraged to allow team members to come up with new ways of achieving the desired outputs and outcomes.

The relationship between the project constraints and the way the project's products are to be delivered has to be considered in the early stages of the project planning.

This is the first example where the standard CPPRRSS sequence is modified (see Figure 2.7). The impact of the time constraint on the choice of processes may affect the product set. For this project, concrete is now an aggregate created using chemically heated components. A tight iteration between product and process is a common experience when 'time is of the essence.'

In a different environment, the patching and completing of plasterboard ceilings using a bucket as a platform might be considered risky, but the risk to the end-date takes priority over the risk to a ricked ankle. Projects are about planning to achieve the desired objective, not a work

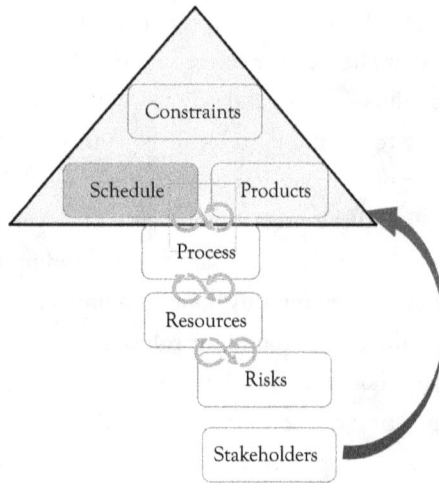

Figure 2.7 The planning steps when time is the top constraint

environment designed to accommodate the worries of the world, though ignoring safety is not a recommended practice.

Fast-Tracking or Crashing the Schedule

Fast-tracking means compressing a schedule, not by working faster or changing processes, but by spreading the work across resources working concurrently, introducing parallel tasks as opposed to serial processing.

Let's consider a simple project: We need to dig a trench, lay a pipe, and then fill in afterward. It takes three days to dig the trench, one day to lay the pipe, and two days to fill in and make neat. So with one person, let's call him Chris, it's going to take six days. You could crack the whip or attempt to incentivize with gifts, but Chris will pretty much take the time it takes him. The situation is set out in Figure 2.8.

Now suppose after a day of digging, Mary starts to lay the pipe in the bit of trench already dug. She'll have some hanging about to do because laying pipe is much quicker than digging. And then there's Ken, who as soon as a length of pipe has been laid fills in and neatens up. He'll also be kept waiting quite a lot, but here's the thing—done right the 'dig, lay, fill' project would be finished in just a little over three days. That's fast-tracking.

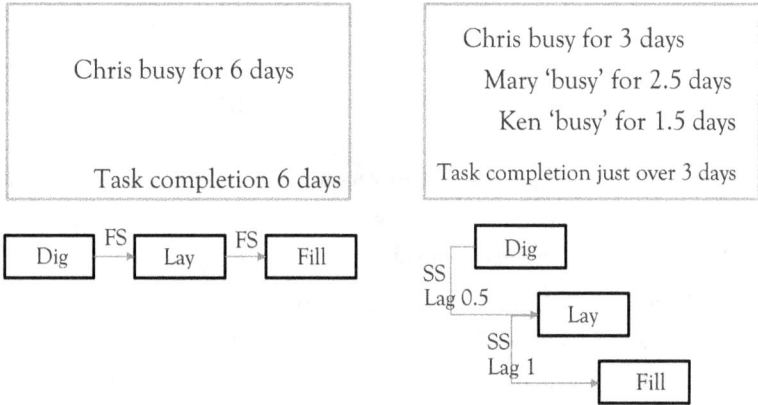

Figure 2.8 Dig-lay-fill

This approach is using a sequencing technique—'SS' links with a lag in a directed network graph (PERT is an example) rather than 'FS' links. See below.

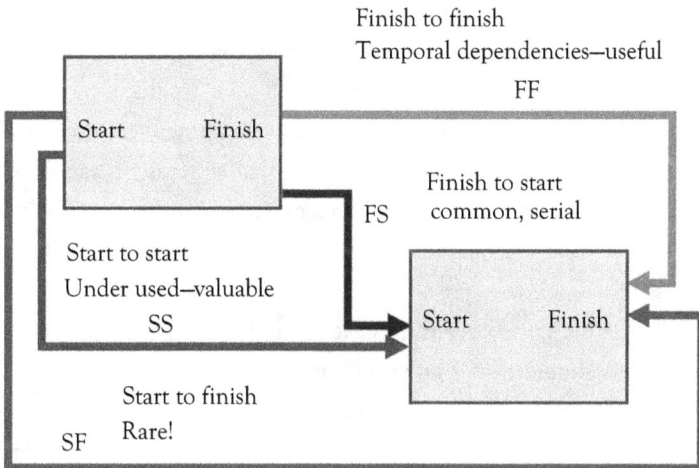

Figure 2.9 Four types of link in a directed network

In the four-hour house, one example of fast-tracking is the roof being built separately and in parallel with the floors and wall going up. Normally the roof would not be started until the walls were up. The roof is then built to fit the walls. Scheduling parallel activities, and doing things in unusual sequences, introduces risks. Building the roof before the walls means that the tolerances for the building of the walls are much tighter—the roof has to fit when it's lowered onto the walls! Another new process and an expensive one is also required—we need a crane with a very skilled crane operator. Once again, the interplay between constraints and processes are influencing the planning process.

Crashing a schedule, adding more resource, does occasionally work, but it is a lot less valuable than inexperienced project managers believe. Just as a thought experiment, how many people can effectively paint the inside of a broom cupboard?

A Detailed Schedule

How often do you use your schedule to determine, dictate even, what your resources will do, hour by hour, minute by minute? It may be no surprise that on the four-hour house project the schedule listed the duration of every activity in great detail. You can see how necessary it might be to keep so many people coordinated.

Perhaps what may be more surprising is the level of detail required to control the transfer-to-operations stage used on a technical project that introduced a new capability to an insurance company. With the business demanding 24/7 availability of its operational systems, it had become increasingly difficult to schedule in major systems upgrades. Table 2.1 is an extract from a schedule controlling the migration of updates to a business-critical IT system.

It had to be done over the weekend, and the plan included a roll-back process should things go wrong. Everything (either the completely recovered old system or the fully functioning new one) had to be up and working on Monday morning—without fail. The level of attention to detail of the scheduling and the intensive communications to ensure the coordinated input from a variety of stakeholders is a perfect example of how planning can support the delivery of capability within tight time constraints.

The plan identified when and where it was necessary to schedule at this level of detail—not all parts of a project will gain any benefit from

Table 2.1 Detailed scheduling of implementing a business-critical system

Event	Comms groups			Description	Method	Time
	ManCo	**Techs**	**Testers**			
Milestone 1 communication	X	X	X	Commencement of physical server shutdown	SMS	07h00
Checkpoint 1		X		Key technical resources to confirm completion of packed physical server and commencement of transportation to CDC per SMS	SMS	09h00
Checkpoint 2 communication		X		Key technical resources to confirm start-up of the physical server at CDC	SMS	10h30
Milestone 2 communication	X	X	X	Environmental update as to physical server delivered and start-up at CDC	SMS	11h00
Checkpoint 4		X		Stand-alone VM storage. Synchronize source and target volumes completed	SMS	12h00
Checkpoint 5		X		Un-map storage mappings in DC2 completed for standalone systems	SMS	13h00
Milestone 4 communication	X	X	X	Environmental update as to physical server installation completed successfully at CDC	SMS	14h00
And so on until final go/no-go decision						
Checkpoint 9	X	X	X	Go/no-go decision	Conference call	21h01

this approach. An obvious problem when micro-scheduling is that any delay or acceleration will cause the timing and sometimes the sequence to become invalid. One of the genuinely brilliant aspects of the planning of the four-hour house was that the detailed schedule not only included start times, and finish times but it also dealt with how to handle delays and opportunities—events that occur that provide earlier-than-expected completed tasks. Opportunity management—the opposite of risk management—is a genuine, if somewhat underused, discipline in project management. In the context of scheduling, it is how to implement 'as soon as possible' (ASAP) scheduling, without dislocating the sequencing of tasks and introducing non-productive 'wait' states.

What Do We Mean by End-Date?

For the four-hour house, giving an end-date was easy; it was later that day! Project managers, when asked, will usually volunteer an end-date, or a 'completion' date, for example, August. Incidentally, when pressed, it always seems that it is the end of the month. The truth is, however, that less than 20 percent of projects are genuinely end-date driven. The dates given are not deadlines: they are either:

- *Estimated dates*: baseline finish dates that have been calculated based on a task-sequencing tool. These vary over the life of the project as the level of certainty around what is to be delivered and how long the tasks will take, fluctuates
- *Target dates*: a date agreed with the sponsor as a target, but with the understanding that it can be renegotiated should it become necessary to do so. Targets are not constraints—unless, of course, the sponsor makes them so.

And this is important! The target date may be regarded as a deadline, but it is not treated as a drop-dead end-date. It is not the primary driver as it is not at the apex of the hierarchy of constraints. It will, therefore not be the factor driving the behavior and approach of the project manager.

When we were researching the characteristics of successful project managers, we found that high-performing project managers (HPGs) were acutely aware of what the constraints were on their project, and adapted their approach and planning techniques accordingly.

For example, when scheduling time-constrained projects, HPGs worked backwards from the end-date rather than forwards from the start date. They found it more helpful to recursively ask, "When do I have to finish by?" than to try to develop optimum schedules and then apply constraints to provide the working schedule. They would also ask, "Can we deliver the scope with the current processes and resources?" If the answer to this question was "No," then they would revisit the plan and adjust the processes or the scope, rather than making often infeasible and unsupportable assumptions about productivity and completion rates to make the schedule work.

Time-constrained projects can be tough on teams; they may involve hard work and lots of overtime. However, our research suggests that managerially, they are often less complex. With an understood, agreed and, most importantly, an immovable constraint—a genuine drop-dead deadline end-date—the compromises that have to be made are clear-cut. Either you meet the end-date—or you fail. It is much easier to manage when the conditions of success are clear.

Project managers can sometimes become typecast. For some, all the projects they do are end-date driven, or they think all projects are end-date driven. Either way, they adopt a single style and a single approach, and it can get them into trouble.

In one notable case, we tracked an IT project manager who had completed three successful time-constrained projects in a row. With such a track record, she was the obvious first choice for a most important project. This project, however, was not time-constrained. Its critical success factor—its topmost constraint—was creating and maintaining intensive collaboration with several business stakeholders.

She struggled and struggled with this project and was eventually taken off it. In the lessons-learned review, it became apparent that she had continued to plan and use a style, which had worked well for her on the previous projects—"We have to get it done in this time frame." However, that just was not the case on this project. The sponsor knew that the project's success depended on active and willing engagement from important stakeholders. As for timing, as far as the sponsor was concerned, today would be fine, or tomorrow; but in fact, whatever the date was when the stakeholders reached a consensus was the right date. The project manager did not understand how to do that, or how to plan a project that had to reflect the voice of the stakeholders. Her approach and her planning style were directive and forceful: necessary to drive forward time-constrained project, not so useful when creating collaborative alliances.

Recognizing a Time-Constrained Project

Time-constrained projects arise from four external drivers:

- *Window-of-opportunity*—the value of completing the project is severely compromised if delivery is late, for example producing a game for the Christmas market
- *Compliance*—meeting a legislated delivery date, for instance becoming compliant with new privacy laws for personal data
- *End-of-life*—increased risk of unprotected catastrophic failure caused by using systems and products after their predicted shelf-life, for example using obsolete switching gear
- *Public commitments*—exposing the organization to public ridicule or genuine reputational risk, for example, the opening event of the Olympic Games

In each of these cases, the significance of meeting the end-date varies depending upon the sponsor's view of the risk exposure, or loss of benefit, they are prepared to countenance. Missing a legislative compliance date may result in a fine, but the sponsor may decide that this is preferable to the additional costs associated with speeding up the delivery of the project. In a time-constrained project, the project manager must understand the sponsor's position about the date.

There is a fifth cause of time-constrained projects. It's called timeboxing.

Noticing the often-useful management effects of rigidly maintained time constraints on projects some software development methodologies—notably DSDM and RAD—adopted the imposition of rigid time constraints on the product development process.

In the right circumstances and for the right products, a time-boxed approach works. Its value arises from the impact on what management is obliged to implement to meet its obligations driven by the temporal constraint. Done well, and using the time constraint as a driver for innovation in tasking and resourcing, it is a powerful productivity tool.

Implemented poorly, the time constraint becomes an excuse for de-scoping with disappointing results. There are many circumstances where the imposition of an unnecessary time-constraint leads to trouble, including situations where incurring the associated technical debt is unacceptable. Whatever else it may be, timeboxing is not a panacea for every project.

Strategies for Planning Time-Bound Projects

As we see in the four-hour house, where an end-date must be met, the planning process changes. The standard product-to-process stepwise elaboration is not productive. These two need to be considered together in a close iteration, mediated by the impact that the candidate processes have on elapsed time. Planning under time constraints always demands more effort in planning, not less. It is essential, therefore, that the project manager engages with the stakeholders so that they become aware of this and in so doing resists the just 'get on with it' pressure so often applied by them.

Table 2.2 summarizes time-constrained project planning strategies. If 'time is of the essence' for your project; if you need to bring in your project in tight time-scales, use this as a checklist of actions.

Table 2.2 Possible time-constrained project planning strategies

Strategy	Tactics
'Crash' the schedule—add resources	Working with larger numbers of resources influences the way work is structured, scheduled, and communicated. Model activities and allocations to make sure you can apply these resources productively. Remember the bigger the team resources; the less productive each member will be. And, more resources and more tasks mean greater monitoring

(Continued)

Table 2.2 (Continued)

Strategy	Tactics
Identify elapsed time delays, those activities which are not compressible using existing processes	Develop new processes, which allow products to be delivered faster. Process experts may not be your best source—they tend to be naysayers. Remember new procedures will create new types of errors, and you won't have prepared ways to correct them. So test and monitor more
Identify delays which may be introduced because of decision making processes	Ensure clarity on who makes what decisions and stick to it. Factor in decision making; bring governance closer to the project. Delayed issue resolution is likely to kill your project
Fast-track the schedule—look for ways of breaking dependencies between activities	Evaluate and manage the additional risks associated with changing the standard dependency structures. Identify management actions and include in plans. Parallel tasks increase resources and risks, so increase monitoring. Remember to investigate Start-to-Start with lag times sequencing rather the Finish-to-Start serial sequencing
Identify resource skills gaps up front	Whenever a task demands effort from a *specific* resource, spend the time to try to eliminate it—it is a significant risk on time-constrained projects. If that is not possible, make the attaining and managing of that person as a CSF for the project
Communicate and re-communicate the purpose, objective, CSFs, and value of the project throughout the project's lifecycle	Find ways in meetings and one-on-ones to rehearse the mission of the project with every member of the project team—and in the steering group—and keep checking back with the sponsor that nothing has changed
Identify foreseeable problems (risks)	No risk statement should be logged unless there is at least one management action associated with it. Most 'fix-on-failure' solutions will cost more in time and money than the other four risk strategies. In time-constrained projects, making good is the least favored option
Be prepared for unforeseen problems	Schedule milestones, and if necessary inch pebbles. Only schedule at the level of detail that reflects your level of uncertainty. The less you know, the greater the detail! Remember schedules are the most volatile project document. Expect to change it frequently to account for the unplanned circumstances

Reflections

It is likely that most of you reading this will have been exposed to a time-bound project, even if it wasn't quite a four-hour house! Consider for your projects:

1. When planning a time-constrained project do you have an option to negotiate the end-date? If it really is immovable, what is the reason: window-of-opportunity, compliance, end-of-life, public commitment, or something else?
2. Have you used any of the strategies described in Table 2.2? Are there any others you have found useful when managing time-constrained projects?
3. If you have used Agile as a development approach, do you consider timeboxing to be a way of controlling effort, or stimulating creativity? What additional risks are caused when applying rigid time-constraints to a project?
4. What techniques do you find most useful when monitoring a time-constrained project? Does your plan support this easily? How different are these from those you use in other types of projects?
5. When scheduling time-constrained projects, which of these approaches do you find useful, and in what ways?
   (a) Effort-time analysis and sequencing of tasks
   (b) Calendar-time sequencing of tasks
   (c) Dependency graphing using:
     • FS, SS, FF, SF (S = Start F = Finish)
   (d) Critical chain
   (e) Gantt charting

CHAPTER 3

Resource-Driven Planning

While it is tempting to assume that limited resource is a subset of a cost constraint-sometimes it just isn't. If you only have access to five people and a cat, then a project planned for six pairs of hands is not going to work! At least not in the way you thought it would. The simple fact is that money and resources are rarely as interchangeable as sponsors like to believe. As we see in the following examples, sometimes no matter how much money you have, the resources—whether it be people or physical assets—are just not available.

Planning Around Scarce Resources

The change of signaling technology from analog to digital was implemented to improve the safety and throughput of trains on the East Coast mainline track in the UK. Critical to the project was the ability to prove that the new signaling system was safe and that there could not be any 'live-side' failures. Getting it 'about right' was unacceptable; peoples' lives were at stake. The process for testing was well defined and non-negotiable. The only people who could execute and sign off the tests were called first principle signal engineers and were very special–you could not go out and rustle up a few more, no matter how much budget was released.

The rail authorities had set a provisional completion date, but nobody knew whether the testing could be completed by then. There was a strong temptation to just get on with it, but it was a very public project, and a large number of stakeholder groups had legitimate interests in its progress. The railway authority needed to be able to tell the railway operators a firm end-date so that they had time to respond and to advise the public of the new train timetables. The project needed a commitment-to-readiness that had a high probability of being achieved.

So was this a project where the critical constraint was time? Absolutely not! Safety was paramount, and could not be sacrificed in the name of expediting completion. Was it, in fact, the kind of project where the fundamental constraint is fulfilling a specific requirement in a particular way? That was tempting, and indeed planning had begun on that basis. Under that kind of constraint, the project would need to be planned and managed as discussed in Chapter 5. But the operational imperative of knowing when the work was to be completed worried the senior project manager involved. He knew that providing gold-plated assurances as to end-dates does not feature in the planning of such projects. So, he wondered, what was the fundamental constraint?

The determining factor when establishing the completion date was the rate of clearance of signals, and that was carried out by, and could only be carried out by the first principle signaling engineers, and it was their availability that limited throughput. This insight stopped the planning process, as it would lead the project down the wrong path. This project needed to be planned as a resource-constrained project.

Armed with the evidence that signal testing was the most critical activity in the project, the project manager persuaded the project board of the importance of planning around the resources—not the outputs, not the tasks, but the resource—and more specifically these scarce or 'golden' resources: first principle signaling engineers.

When a category of resource is the constraint, the best approach is to deal with them not as resources but as assets. They are the generators of future value in the project schedule. They need to be ring-fenced, protected from lower-value tasks, and never be kept waiting for work. The supply to them needs to be managed and sequenced as the throughput of the whole project is determined by the throughput of this resource.

The result is that the scarce resources are 'leveled'; reducing peaks of usage, and scheduled to near a hundred percent utilization.

Leveling is defined by the PMI as a technique in which start and finish dates are adjusted, based on resource constraints with the goal of balancing demand for resources with the available supply.

It might sound simple, but in practice, it isn't. To be effective, leveling may require activities that seem to be unitary to be split. Parallel activities have to be enabled and managed, sometimes forcing the implementation of such unusual scheduling practices as finish-to-finish sequencing. The purpose is to optimize the allocation of the scarce resource. Sometimes it can lead to physically impractical solutions, and it usually requires a detailed understanding of the specifics of the activity.

The project management task was now to establish two things that were at that time unknowns. What was the clearance rate for a tested-as-safe signal? And, how many signals needed to be tested? Questions not asked before and not necessary to ask in a project planned under mission-critical criteria. Finding this information, establishing an inventory and a 'job card' for processing the items in it, sounds straightforward but it took many iterations to eliminate the phrase "I think" from the vocabulary of the project. "I think it took me 2 hours." "I think there are 23 signals in that segment." "I think I can clear these signals this week." When you are responsible for the delivery of a project based on through-put, you do need to know–for sure.

When the answer was finally known, it turned out completion would not be in November as the rail authority had suggested initially, and it would not be the following March that the harassed signaling project manager had promised. It would be the following September because that was how long it would take with the first principle signaling engineers available to the project to clear the 4,318 signals.

The problem of communicating this September go-live date to the by now punch drunk railway operators, who had been seeing end-dates come and go, and then to the public, was handled magnificently. Rather than explain what might appear as poor project planning, the external stakeholders were advised that the summer timetables would be continued throughout the winter and into the following summer, in response to suggestions from the traveling public. Everyone liked that.

The project was delivered at the re-baselined end-date and hailed as a success by all the stakeholder groups. It is a good demonstration of how upfront planning, focused on the right constraint, allowed the project to deliver to its success criteria–a firm end date, and no signaling incidents.

Resource-constrained projects do not follow the standard CPPRRSS planning sequence. The steps are illustrated in Figure 3.1. Resources and the processes they can deploy effectively are tightly bound together, and

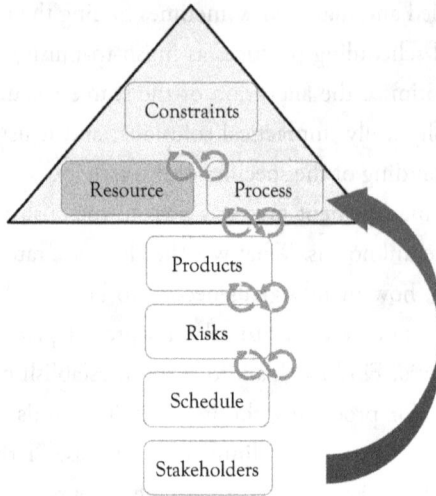

Figure 3.1 Planning in resource-constrained projects

there is rapid iteration between them. The critical information is productivity, in this case, the rate of clearance. (It is worth noting here that when the processes chosen are highly skilled resources carrying out intellectually demanding tasks, the project manager needs to establish additional interim and management products to allow monitoring of progress—see Figure 1.4 on components of a PBS for an explanation of interim and management products.)

Making Resource Demands Visible

In the rail-signaling project, the first principle signal engineers would always be the bottleneck. The sensible thing to do was, therefore, to manage them as golden resources. On some projects, the bottleneck resource varies, with different work-packages relying on different types of scarce resources. Planning under these circumstances becomes a matter of structuring sets of tasks around resource availability, rather than a logical sequencing of activities.

High Speed 1 (HS1) was the UK's first high-speed rail linking London to the European network. It was also the first new British railway in 100 years and the UK's largest-ever single construction project. The program had 80 work streams at its peak, but the real complexity came from the delicate balancing of political, corporate, and environmental interests; moving services across London; building and decamping to a new depot; and most importantly taking staff and passengers on the journey from the old service location in Waterloo to the new one at St Pancras.

Every business unit in Eurostar was involved in the program as well as many external partners and suppliers. Existing operational services had to continue undisturbed during the program execution. So, the staff was asked to contribute to the program while pursuing their day job. The challenge for the project was to create credible, transparent and agreed-to work demands. The planners had to be sure who needed whom, and when, and to communicate this information in two directions; to the individuals and the project planners.

Table 3.1 is an extract from one of the resource impact charts used to assess resource 'hot spots.' It is an analysis of the organizational breakdown structure against the proposed work streams for the program. What it highlighted was, not when people were needed–that is ordinary scheduling–but when tasks and activities could be done because key people were available then. This is using resource management as the driver of your schedules.

Limited Resources Demand Different Options

Even when the resource is neither specialist nor particularly difficult to find it can still become scarce when there is competition for it, a situation that is uncomfortably familiar to many project managers. Moreover, it does not have to be people in short supply.

The FIFA football world cup took place in South Africa in 2010– in the build-up and the two years following the games South Africa struggled to source enough bitumen for its road construction projects. (Bitumen is a by-product of oil refining and is used to produce asphalt for road surfacing.)

The situation is dire and is significantly impacting the industry. It is not just large construction and asphalt companies that are being affected, but small companies too, which is having a ripple effect on other business sectors…[particularly] in the road-building

Table 3.1 Identifying critical resources (extract from Eurostar resource plan)

Workstream	Projects or primary products	IT	Legal	Commercial	Distribution	Comms	Engineering
Distribution density	GDS in UK (2.5)			dedicated	dedicated		
	Cross partition ticketing	dedicated		participation	participation		
Share of wallet	Journey plus enhancements	dedicated		dedicated			
Business intelligence	Eurostar business intelligence	dedicated					
IT infrastructure renewal	IT infrastructure renewal	dedicated					
Intranet	Intranet	consult				dedicated	
Commercial workstreams	Image and brand values			consult			
	International GDS access (GSA/BSP)			dedicated	consult		
	Internet portal connections to the Eurostar reservation system (ERS)			dedicated			
Operations workstreams	Interfaces between French and UK train maintenance systems	dedicated					consult
	Maintenance scheduling process across the fleet						dedicated
	Specialization of the workload at individual depots						dedicated

Legend: Need to consult on solutions | Need participation | Need dedicated resources

*industry–the South African Roads Agency reported that 35 major
road projects had been severely delayed by the shortage.*

—SA Bitumen Association

Many projects languished. Planned on the basis that resources would be available when the need arose for them–one of the most common assumptions made by project managers–they had stalled when the bitumen was not forthcoming. Other projects, using planning techniques that were based on the availability of the scarcest resource, did better.

Having identified that completion would be impacted by bitumen shortages; the companies running these projects initiated early actions to source alternative locally available paving products and got them approved. A series of risk management actions triggered and justified by the planning approach that prioritized resources.

There is one function in today's industry that has a habit of creating highly competed-for resources; IT. Currently, particularly in the retail sector, but also more generally, the demand for SAP specialist skills is driving up contract rates, delaying projects, and frustrating businesses. The response by some is to look for alternative solutions, and alternative technologies, driven, not by dissatisfaction with the SAP solution, but by the constraints put on them by scarce resources.

More Resource!

One of the reasons why the early Star War films have lasted so well is that though fantastical; there are many recognizable parallels with our world. Darth Vader, the scary adjutant of the sponsor of the project to build the Death Star, visits the project to check on progress. The project manager, when challenged, nervously exclaims, "I need more men!" Somethings never change.

More resource is a frequent project manager refrain, but it is not always well-founded. Consider the CECA project:

It is early February, and it has come to the attention of the PMO that all is not as it should be with the project. Up until now, based on status reports, for the past 20 weeks, the project appeared to be on track, see Figure 3.2. All planned tasks had been completed, albeit at a higher than

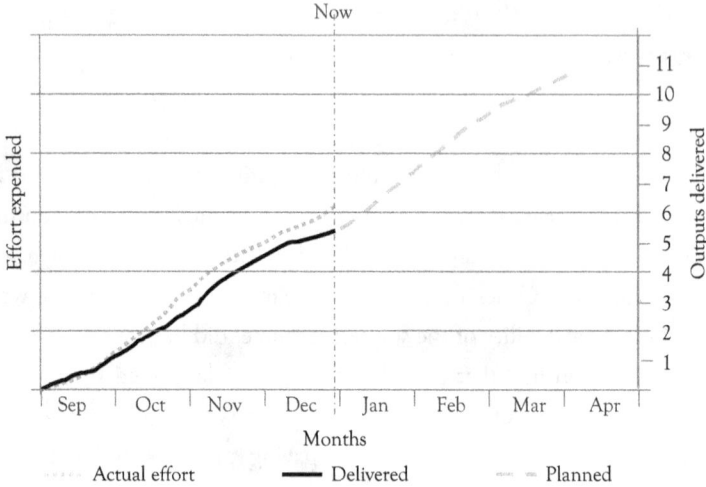

Figure 3.2 The reported performance to date

expected cost. This was due; it was noted, because one of the resources was consistently taking 50 percent more effort to complete her tasks than anticipated, probably because the estimates had been prepared with more experienced, and therefore more productive, staff in mind.

Testing *must* start on 14 April to meet the release date; this is not optional. With 10 elapsed weeks to go, the resource plan showed 74 effort days available. The problem that the PMO had picked up was that the outstanding change requests had increased the scope of the project (the number of outputs required) by an additional 25 percent, which meant that the effort demand was now 111 effort days, taking it well past the required end-date. So, the real situation, when plotted, looked like Figure 3.3: the planned curve was now *above* the delivered curve, so the project was no longer showing that it was on track. By extrapolating the delivered curve–the dotted black line in Figure 3.3—it is clear that, at that rate of productivity, delivering all the outputs would make the project late.

The PMO sat down with the project manager to discuss options.

Naturally, seeing the problem as a resource shortfall, the project manager asked for more resource. The PMO pointed out two facts: the project manager hadn't dealt with the resources he already had particularly well, as at no stage was the under-productivity of the team addressed, and secondly, with only 10 weeks to go, there just wasn't time for someone to be recruited, inducted and made productive to make enough of a difference.

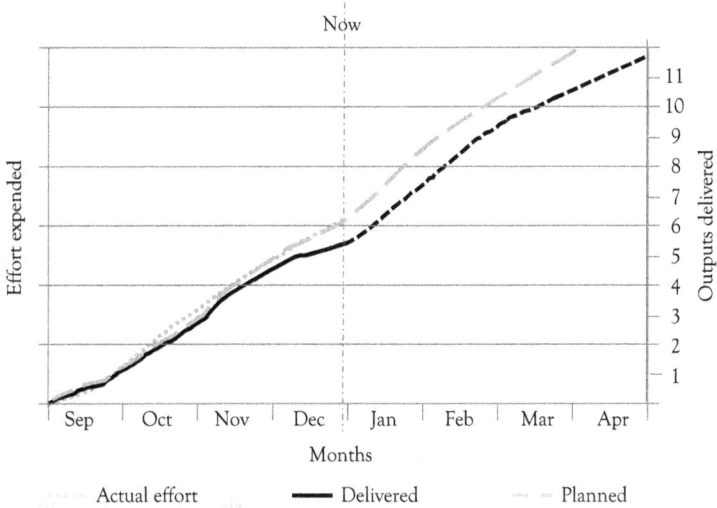

Figure 3.3 The real state of affairs

"What other options are there?" the project manager asked. Delaying the start of testing was not an option. One or two calendar days overrun might not prove disastrous, but the business dates posed an immovable barrier. And warming to his task, he pointed out, given the significant increase in scope during the first two-thirds of the project; some contingency had to be built in to absorb further increases.

He could, he supposed, reschedule, changing the allocation of tasks and crashing the schedule. On its own, though, these actions were unlikely to give sufficient extra productivity, or enough contingency to guarantee completion dates.

"What about re-scoping the project?" the PMO manager finally suggested. A cursory examination of the project mission identified that a few of the products did not have to be delivered by the testing deadlines, and enough of them to make a big enough difference. And, provided a rapid follow-on project was initiated to implement them, the additional costs imposed on the business would be bearable.

For this option to have any merit, however, it had to be sanctioned immediately. It would necessitate a re-plan, and a reschedule—to stop work on the now non-essential aspects—and it had to be agreed by the sponsor and key stakeholders, including the CEO. The options were presented to them as shown in Figure 3.4.

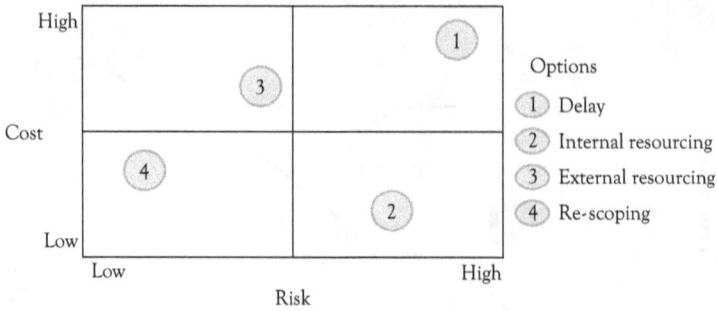

Figure 3.4 The options—cost vs. risk

No one chose 'more resource.'

CECA is a project that we have used many, many times on our courses and workshops. The vast majority of even experienced project managers select the 'more resource' option, and we wonder why? In CECA, the interaction between low productivity and increase in scope is often over-looked in the hunt for a single silver bullet. The focus of attention of the project managers tends to be on activities and staff allocation, while the answer lies partly in dealing with project productivity of the team and of an individual; and more particularly further back, in the project mission itself. More resource, particularly in the later stages of a project, is rarely the best option!

When the Team Is Fixed

There is yet another way in which projects can be constrained, sometimes unintentionally, by the lack of resource required to deliver the project.

Many project managers, particularly running internal projects, find themselves managing 'rectangular' effort curves. That is to say, even though projects have known and predictably changing demands for resources over time, most project managers run a team of a fixed size. The characteristic shape of the required effort from project teams was shown to follow Rayleigh's curve in work done by Slim and Putnam on work-force build-up (MBI) in projects (see Figure 3.5).

Running fixed teams can lead to productivity problems, but they are not the subject of this discussion. What is; is how to manage the resource availability-constraint that running a fixed team might impose?

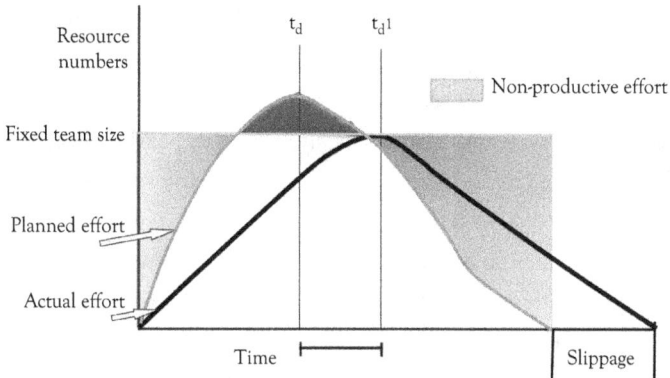

Figure 3.5 The Slim-Putnam curve

The Slim-Putnam curve describes the level of productive effort required to deliver a project. When you superimpose the available effort from a fixed team, you get graphs similar to that shown in Figure 3.5. What it shows is that during the early stages it is difficult to engage the team members fully, as tasks are not 'available' for them to apply effort and this is also true as the project begins to wind down. The shaded areas under the 'fixed team size' line represent paid-for-labor that does not result in *valuable* project work. In such situations project managers can become distracted, finding work for team members, which may end up actually impeding work necessary for project completion.

The point 't_d' is the point of maximum resource demand. For this project, and with this fixed team size, the resource available is less than the amount of effort required, which results in the peak moving to the right 't_{d1},' and that causes end-date slippage. It is quite a well-known story to many project managers. Adding resource in an attempt to hasten the completion of a project is a good a way of delaying it. To finish a project you need to shut tasks down, not open new ones.

The second problem with fixed teams is more to do with managing capability than capacity. Experienced project managers realize that there is no point in planning a solution that the individuals on the team are ill-equipped to deliver. When you have access to the necessary skills, it is appropriate to plan for the best technical solution. Otherwise, the plan needs to set out what is managerially best, which involves structuring the work so that both the effort time and the calendar time are predictable.

Of course, there is a downside to modifying solutions to suit the available skills, which is why unintentionally imposing resource constraints is not such a good idea. Several years ago, a large financial company ring-fenced specialist IT and financial analyst resources and dedicated them to their business transformation programs. The early successes and extra pace they achieved turned, within a couple of years, into staleness and sameness as new problems and new opportunities were solved using the same set of solutions. This fixed team approach was abandoned as a failed experiment after four years.

A useful insight into project teams comes from work done on the impact of turnover on a project. Research on the factors that affect project productivity found that increased churn rates negatively affected project performance. So, you are not surprised. The interesting finding is that a small amount of turnover increased productivity! (See Figure 3.6.)

What would cause that? Well, it turned out that when a new member joined the team, the project manager, and the team revisited, rehearsed, and re-communicated the project mission, what the project was for–what its purpose was, who was contributing to what, and what the status of the project was. The accidental value of this was that it refreshed the project

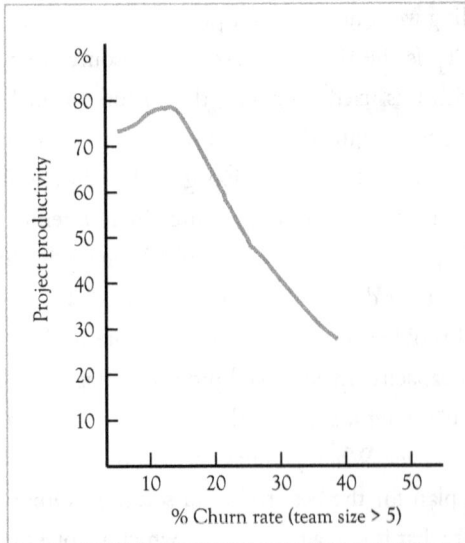

Figure 3.6 *Impact of churn rate on project productivity*

team's understanding, and their perspectives and roles were re-invigorated. It makes you wonder if doing this by chance were so valuable, what would the gain be if it were done deliberately?

One of the strengths of some Agile teams is that the members do have daily meets; they do share a common picture and make use of techniques they are well versed in—a genuine team environment. There is, however, a distinct possibility of a similar unintentional resource-based constraint being applied as experienced by the financial services program team. The skills combination within the team, in the end, determines the set of solutions, and the sequence of delivery and in so doing detaches delivery from the reality of business-driven needs.

When Project Managers Are the Problem

A banking group had recognized that its IT portfolio of projects was stalled. Projects made it onto the portfolio register, but would then not progress for months, if ever. What was the cause and how could throughput be increased?

Over the period of a year, there were between 40 and 60 projects in the portfolio. The portfolio register showed that there were 22 project managers managing between one and three project-starts a year. (In this sector, with IT-intensive projects, this is about average, depending on the level of skill of the project manager.)

Although the total number of project managers looked about right, on closer inspection of the nature of the portfolio it became apparent that there were insufficient PM2 (medium experience) and PM3 (high experience) project managers, see Figure 3.7.

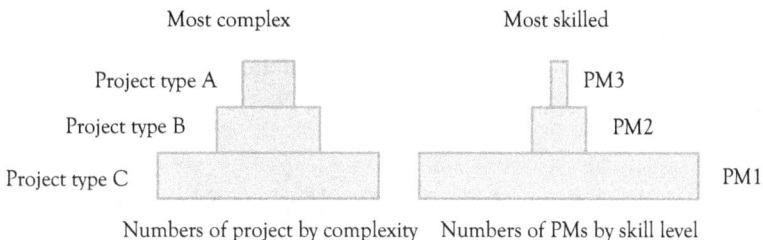

Figure 3.7 The mismatch between the profiles of projects and project managers

Table 3.2 Strategies to cope with PM/portfolio mismatch

Strategy	Impact time	Challenges/risks
Reduce the number of projects	Short-medium term	Governance processes need to be improved to ensure fast decisions about project priorities
Make projects less complex	Medium term	Skilled portfolio analysts required to break down projects. Improved portfolio management (in particular interdependency management) required
Recruit	Short term	Increased costs and potential for tensions with existing staff if too many contract staff brought in. Increased induction and management overhead to deal with new staff intakes
Re-skill	Medium-long term	Loss of project effort to training time, coaching and mentoring time. Skills may still be lacking

Type 2 projects (classified through an analysis of size and complexity) were being assigned to PM1 (low experience, junior) project managers who lacked the skills, behavior, and attitudes to drive these more complex projects.

To improve the throughput of projects in the portfolio, a number of strategies are possible. The number of projects in the portfolio could be reduced, or made much simpler in structure and scope. Alternatively, the skills of the project managers would need to be raised through training and/or recruitment. The four basic strategies are set out in Table 3.2.

The banking group used a combination of the four strategies. First, they had mapped the project interdependencies–how one project affected others in the portfolio. Then they had the projects restructured, splitting or aggregating them to simplify and reduce the number of dependencies, making the projects more 'do-able' by the project managers that they had. They also eased the time constraints on some projects, and where it proved difficult to reduce the complexity, provided coaching and mentoring to less experienced project managers working on projects that were assessed as 'challenging.'

And Sometimes It's the Project Sponsor

While we were sorting this problem out, it became clear that there was another issue lurking near the surface. One of the resources commonly

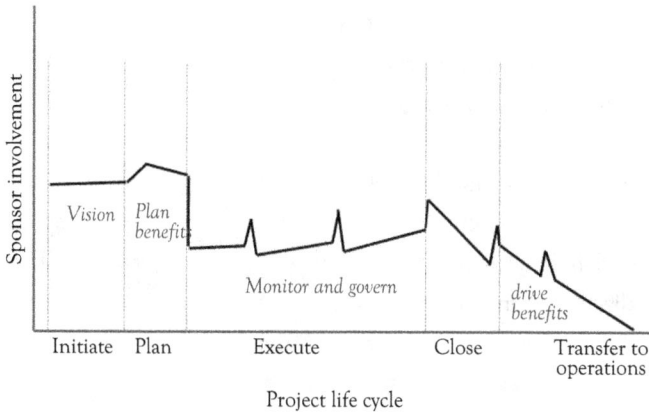

Figure 3.8 Involvement of the project sponsor

under-valued in projects is access to stakeholders, and in particular, access to the project sponsor.

The level of commitment of the sponsor to a project will vary by the nature of the project, but it also varies considerably over the lifetime of a project (Figure 3.8).

In general, the peak period when attention is required from the sponsor is in the initiation and planning stages of the project. Because of the annual planning cycle in this banking company, project-starts bunched together at the beginning of the year. This resulted in particularly high demands for sponsor activity, which was neither anticipated nor serviced. This was another reason why projects got onto the portfolio register but were often delayed for several months in initiation.

All the projects in the IT portfolio of the bank had a sponsor, but there were only five sponsors for the 60 projects, giving an average of 12 projects per sponsor. As it happened, one of the sponsors was the CEO, and he was the sponsor of 19 projects. Seen as an advantage by the project managers to have such a powerful sponsor for their project, it wasn't. They never got to see him!

Under the circumstances, it was considered apolitical to confront the CEO with this issue, so we ran some workshops to debate the following questions:

1. How many projects are you sponsoring?

2. What has the role of the sponsor been in those projects?
3. What project actions have been triggered by sponsor interactions in the past three months?

The atmosphere in the early workshops was distinctly frosty as it became increasingly clear to the individuals charged with sponsoring projects that they had no idea what was expected of them. They had not realized how much time was involved, nor how varied the types of interactions expected of them were. In the third workshop, the CEO of the bank stood up and took charge, saying

> *Here we are investing millions, and we haven't got time to take respon-*
> *sibility for it! From now on, I will accept the stewardship of no more*
> *than three projects. If the other projects can't find someone who cares*
> *enough, let them wait, or die a natural death.*

and swept our. They say leadership comes from the top, and, in this bank, the impact of the CEO's attitude toward sponsorship was immediate and enormously positive. The bank took forward four actions:

• All sponsors to be inducted into the role to ensure they were aware of the commitment required.
• Start projects when and only when business sponsorship can commit the time for engagement.
• Monitor the portfolio demand for critical resources.
• Stagger the start of projects to optimize the project resources, including sponsors' time, available.

The combination of the restructuring of projects and the realistic scheduling of projects against the availability of appropriately skilled resources allowed the banking portfolio to address the bottlenecks in their project delivery.

Here we see the impact of project resources on the throughput of projects. In the rush to start projects, it is tempting to assume that the resources will mysteriously become available, but they don't!

Reflections

How do you know when you are dealing with a project where the top-most constraint is a resource? The answer lies in the way risk arising from the use of resources, is treated.

When the conditions of success of the project demand access to a particular, possibly scarce, resource, the resource is not a project risk. It is a constraint (or CSF) and is an integral part of the plan; there are no alternatives. This is the case in projects like the East Coast mainline signaling project and the bitumen projects in South Africa discussed in this chapter. Under these circumstances, the planning process focuses on the following four tactics:

- Monitoring and control of 'golden resources'
- Resource scheduling—leveling
- Investment in the development of alternative resources
- Designing the project around the resource

This situation contrasts sharply with those projects where, in the process of planning, you choose to use a specific resource. Under those circumstances, the use of the resource often is a risk and therefore is subject to additional management actions, a plan B so as to speak.

Then there are projects where it is not that you don't have the right resources, it's just that there are no more resources available for the project. What are the options now? The typical way to deal with limited resource availability is resource leveling, a technique that has the merit of simplicity but is a brute-force tool with little subtlety.

Consider for your projects:

1. Most project managers have felt they could do with more resource at some point. Which approaches have you made work?
2. When your project involves scheduling heavily competed-for resources, did you find yourself having to make compromises in the planning and scheduling? If so, how did you go about doing that?
3. Have you ever constructed a risk tree to explain the options to a stakeholder or team member? When facing a resource shortfall,

whether it is staff, materials, or money, set up a risk tree to help identify the consequences of the way you intend to deal with the problem.

4. What types of allowances do you make when planning when you are obliged to use non-ideal or even unsuitable resources for some of the tasks?

5. When planning in a resource-constrained project and the resources are not co-located, why is the optimum approach to allocate complete work packages to a location?

CHAPTER 4

Not a Penny More— Budget-Constrained Planning

We don't own the budget, but we are expected to develop it.
Our estimates become the budget for the project.
The budget is pre-set by the client—we just work to it.
We have a target budget, but the client always seems able to find additional money.
We only worry about capital expenditure and external resources; we don't budget for internal resources.
We don't use budgets!

These are a selection of remarks made to us when discussing planning with project managers. None is particularly healthy, displaying a lack of understanding of the purpose and role of a budget in a project by the project manager, the sponsor, and sometimes by both.

In this chapter, we examine why this might be, how to fix it, and when it is vital to know whether the constraint at the top of the hierarchy is money.

Setting the Budget

It has always amused us when business cases set out the costs down to the nearest cent with the benefits rounded to the nearest hundred thousand dollars. This specious accuracy in presenting costs belies the truth. Often there is as much uncertainty about what will be spent, as in the forecast value of the benefits.

A glance at the findings from just one industry, Rail, hammers this point home. Flyvbjerg et al. (2003) investigated the cost-benefit analyses

Table 4.1 *Forecast and actual traffic in the first year*

Project	Actual traffic/predicted traffic (%)
Calcutta Metro, India	5
Miami Metro, USA	15
Channel Tunnel, UK, France	18
Paris Nord TGV line, France	25
Humber Bridge, UK	25
Tyne and Wear Metro, UK	50
Mexico City Metro	50
Denver International airport, USA	55

of many road and rail projects: the message is unequivocal, don't trust them! As they scathingly advise decision makers:

> *Take with a grain of salt any traffic forecast that does not explicitly take into account the risk of being very wrong. For rail passenger forecasts and especially for urban rail, a grain of salt may not be enough.*

Table 4.1 shows the level of accuracy achieved when forecasting benefits (they would say footfall or traffic) from completing the project. The percentages give you some idea, but when you remember that the predicted numbers were in hundreds of thousands, if not millions, it is a huge 'miss.'

Table 4.2, is drawn from the same source, and clearly shows that whatever else was driving these road and railway projects; cost was not one of them. Never mind what the political-posturing and public statements said at the time. It is also clear that the planning regimes adopted did not base their decisions and actions on cost-based considerations. Project success was not determined by meeting the cost constraint.

When Cost Is Set by the Value

The first story in this chapter is, in our experience, relatively unusual as the budget was tightly linked to the return to be expected from the project, and was varied as the expected returns were revalued, in many cases downwards!

Table 4.2 Rail construction overruns

Project	Cost overrun (%)
Boston's artery/tunnel project, USA	196
Humber Bridge, UK	175
Boston-Washington-New York rail, USA	130
Great Belt rail tunnel, Denmark	110
Joetsu Shinkansen rail line, Japan	100
Washington Metro, USA	85
Channel Tunnel, UK, France	80
Karlsruhe-Bretten light rail, Germany	80
Mexico City Metro line	60
Tyne and Wear Metro, UK	55
Great Belt link, Denmark's	54

In a significant Digital Delivery Program (DDP) run by a large finance company the basis of the investment—the allocated spend for the project—was to be determined by what could be agreed as the bankable forecast income over a five-year period. A hurdle rate for the return was set. The only thing that now needed to be done was work out what the cumulative value of the income stream would be, and the project budget would be known.

The approach taken was to set a target value—say $700m—for the total new income and then link this value to changes of buying behaviors of the target population. This, in turn, was related to new digital products, portals, and services.

Figures 4.1 and 4.2 illustrate the mapping process. The example chosen is not from the digital project (DPP) as the results of the detailed research done by that project are still confidential, but the general approach is hopefully clear.

In Figure 4.1, the benefit (in this case 'Cost Avoidance') is identified as arising from five impacts or 'significant points of difference' in the operations of this retail chain. The detail below the benefit and each impact show the key performance indicator (KPI), the profile of the predicted value with time, and the period over which the value will be returned. The strict rule is that unless the impacts and benefits are measurable, they are disallowed!

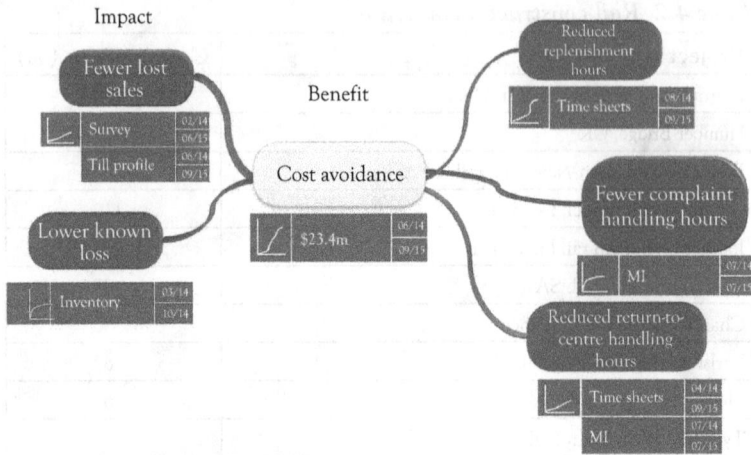

Figure 4.1 Benefits mapping process—step one

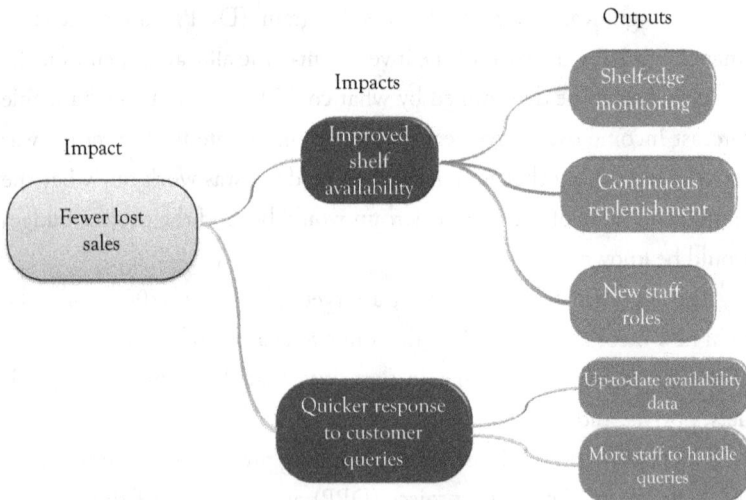

Figure 4.2 Impacts to sub-impacts to products—step two

Figure 4.2 shows one of the impacts being mapped through sub-impacts (and sometimes through sub-sub-impacts, and so on) back to the source of the change, which is usually, as in this case, an output from a project. The impacts are changes in the behavior of people and processes that give rise to the differences in operation. These also have their KPIs and profile.

In this way, there is a chain—a series of links—that can be checked, challenged, and chased. By insisting on having a measure and a target value, and demanding a profile of how and when the change is recognized, the planning gets 'real' for everyone, and arm-waving and vagueness plays a much-reduced role in the specifying of the expected value for a project.

Inevitably, it means that to back up analyses like this you need real data. You also need a commitment from stakeholders that given that the information is valid, they can and will deliver the predicted changes in behaviors. For the DPP it turned out that a surprisingly large number of factors needed to be enumerated and validated. These included the size of the target population, the proportion of that population with smart-phones, the numbers of individuals who buy insurance products, and so on and so on.

In total, 158 parameters—or factors—had to have values associated with them to allow the modeling of the future income to be carried out. Some could be and were researched. Others were harder to deter-mine. These were treated more circumspectly, their less certain values highlighted and their source of validity assigned to one or more of the stakeholders. In this way, the modeling was more transparent, and the stakeholders more involved. It was now their skin in the game.

One of the effects of developing the impact and benefit profiles is that operational managers can visualize how the predicted changes will be realized. It turns out there are only four profiles, with other curves being combinations of them—see Figure 4.3. The 'whoosh' one is universally

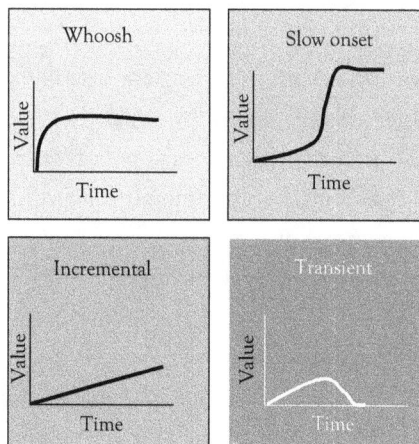

Figure 4.3 Profiles of benefits and impacts over time

liked! It means the impact is immediate, obvious, and sustained. The 'slow-onset' is the commonest profile when profiling IT implementations, with a gradual adoption, a critical mass is reached, and then most everybody else on-boarding after that. The 'incremental' or 'steady Eddy' model is unexciting but valuable as the change progresses, and value is returned, in a possibly slow, but predictable way. The last one, the 'transient' is trouble. Something happens and there is a positive response, but it fades away, energy is lost, and the gains made disappear. Transients can be useful when looking for 'quick wins,' ways of engaging stakeholders, team, and others, but ultimately they return little of value.

As the planning proceeded in the DPP, it became evident that the overall target was too ambitious—the level of benefit-risk was too high to be borne by the stakeholders. And, equally unattractive to many stakeholders; that the contribution made to the income from products and services that had previously not been sold by the company would be more important than had been thought. This needed to be factored into the planning and sequencing of delivery, and the profile of expenditure, because new products carry more risk when predicting future sales than established ones.

What senior management made very clear to the sponsor and project manager was that moving to a digital platform was a commercial rather than a strategic decision. Either the project 'washed its face' and came out clean, or it would be stopped. Coming up clean meant that the project remained financially viable, making an acceptable return on the investment.

So the budget for the project (program actually) was set and, as importantly, the governance process by which it could and would be altered, decided. This is an excellent example of where the cost was a genuine top-level constraint, but the amount changed in-flight. This has a much more benign impact on a project than when the *type* of constraint is changed. In this circumstance, the success criteria haven't changed, just the boundary value.

So why is setting a cost constraint that flexes with the expected return so uncommon? One reason, as is so starkly shown by Tables 4.1 and 4.2 from Flyvbjerg (2003), is that so many business cases—and particularly the benefit cases—are barely worth the paper they are written on.

They often seem to be used to justify a decision already taken rather than as a decision making criterion. Perhaps, more constructively, it may be that it just proves too challenging to get reliable data, or the real value of the return is inadequately captured in purely financial terms.

Another possible reason we encounter frequently is that the concept of value (the price you are willing to pay) gets confused with cost (how much you have to pay). The two are related, but it is a mistake to substitute one for the other.

When It Is the Amount of Money that Matters

The project manager who said, "We have a target budget, but the client always seems able to find additional money" is relating an experience many project managers have had. The reality is that, despite all the rhetoric, budgets are often *not* the constraint—more an aspiration—certainly in government and the larger corporations. Nevertheless, there are some projects, and some environments, where this is most definitely not the case. There are projects where the absolute amount in the budget is a hard ceiling, and the project manager had better know how to deal with it.

The project manager who shared the following story had worked for many years as a program manager running high-spending projects for a large multi-national defense group. When he retired, he was asked to manage a UK lottery-funded project. It was here, for the first time, that he faced the reality of planning a project where the challenge of cost control was as complex as delivering the outputs. How do you plan and execute a project when working within a rigidly defined budget constraint?

The St Edburg's church conservation work in Oxfordshire UK was a project to restore the Grade 1 listed building, parts of which date back 900 years, and was funded by the Heritage Lottery Fund.

The tender process is tightly controlled. A detailed cash flow projection for the project has to be produced, and there are specific criteria as to who can be involved in the budgetary process. For example, the chosen architect must be on the UK conservation register. Where the amounts come from must be documented, and must 'make sense,' and often give rise to complicated financial modeling.

As is standard practice among architects, the project architect's fees were based upon a percentage of the final build price. When forecasting within such a constrained budget, considerations such as 'should you calculate the architect's fees before or after contingency is added to the tender price?' can make the difference between a successful bid—and project failure.

The project went out to tender for the conservation work, knowing what their maximum spend could be. The architect managed the tricky business of advising the construction groups about the budget cap, without actually giving the target figure away. Even so, some of the responses came in at more than double the value of the funding from the Heritage Lottery Fund. Pricing variation like this, occurring in such specialized and tightly specified work, typically means that competition for the right resources is very keen. It is one of the reasons why small pieces of conservation work, such as at St Edburg's, struggle.

The big budget items for the project were the construction fees, the architect's fees, and contingency and management reserve.

Contingency reserves are the estimated costs, which are allocated for identified risks. They are associated with the known-unknowns. The contingency reserve may be a percentage or a fixed cost. They may be aggregated. As more information becomes available, the contingency reserve may be used, reduced, or eliminated.

Management reserves are a specified amount of the project budget withheld for management control purposes and are reserved for unforeseen work. In construction, this figure is often a percentage of the total. Management reserves are intended to address the unknown-unknowns.

On small-budget projects such as St Edburg's, management reserves and contingency are often combined into one figure—in this case; it was set at 10 percent of total fees. There are some technical issues with this approach. For example, contingency is usually managed at the work package level. With a work package completed, any remaining funds should be released—either transferred to the management reserve or removed from the budget. This allows for greater accuracy in the monitoring of costs and cost risk. And there is another problem. Without proper evaluation of the known risk factors, how can you know that 10 percent is enough?

The project manager knew that getting the budget through the Heritage Lottery Funding process was going to be difficult. The supplier they had chosen was right at the top end of their price range, and if too much of the risk money were used, the budget would be exceeded. The request for funding would not be approved if it was even a penny over the target figure. This meant engaging with all the funding and resource groups to come up with an agreed approach:

- The construction group would not include a contingency in their bid—this would reduce their total fees, and the architect's fees.
- The church funding would provide a management reserve— this had to be agreed with the Heritage Lottery Fund group, who typically expect the sponsors to use their funds before getting any lottery money.
- A staged commitment to work was drawn up with the contractor, based on a revised scope. The initial tender had been for three work packages: replacing and repairing damaged stone on the tower; repairs to the north porch; and renewing drainage. It was decided to defer the last work package to another project. It was further agreed that the work on the north porch would only be started once it was clear that sufficient funds remained.

This last point is significant. Grant money is released in three stages, with 50 percent upfront, 40 percent once the first half is completed, and a final 10 percent when all the work has been completed. As the project manager said: "It is very unwise to dismantle anything without being sure that the funds are available for completion, as there is no guarantee that follow-up funding will be made available."

The St Edburg's church restoration project was a success. Not because it did all of the things that had been envisaged in the original scope, but because what was delivered was tightly controlled against what could be afforded. At all times, the stakeholders were kept informed of what could be delivered and how. The focus on budget flavored every decision made by the project manager. "Each time I was asked about doing something better, or different, I had to weigh it against what I knew was left in the budget and what other risks I might need to allow for."

The transparency around the budgetary process affected the behaviors and attitudes of the contractors and stakeholders. For example, the building contractor looked for ways to optimize the utilization of resources. "If we could work on two aspects on the project in parallel I can use some of my free resource time." The stakeholders (the church) recognized the need on some occasions to relax less important constraints: "We will use a different church entrance just for this Sunday so that the project can exploit opportunities for cost containment."

The project exemplifies the impact of an explicit cost constraint: 'not a penny more!' Every aspect of the planning and monitoring—and the decision making processes—were infused with the boundary condition set by the fact that there was no more money. Much like a haiku poem with its rigid limitation on the number of syllables, the immovable constraint led to innovative ways of achieving an outcome, not innovative ways of creating the outputs—that would be far too risky. The learning from this type of project is that constraints do not act to hinder you from achieving your objective, they work to shape the ways you go about achieving it. This case was originally published in the APM's Project magazine (Worsley 2018).

In the case of cost constraints, the planning must enhance and simplify how to monitor expenditure on a day-by-day basis. The reporting must allow stakeholders to access the status of the project—how far away from the end-state the project is—so that they can engage in meaningful actions to support the success of the project, bringing it in within budget.

The Impact on the Planning Process

The two cases discussed earlier are examples of cost-constrained initiatives. In the DPP, what they are prepared to pay is set by what the financial return from the project is worth to the company. Spend beyond that, and the project is a failure. In St Edburg's, the constraint is set externally and is immovable. Where the top most constraint is cost, the planning steps tightly iterate between the products, the processes, and the cost of

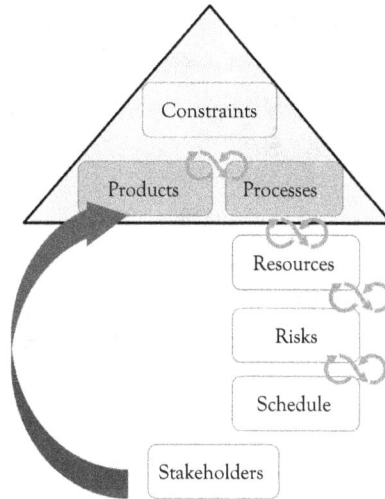

Figure 4.4 Planning sequence in a cost-constrained project

the resources. The answer lies in circumscribing the scope—the set of products—that can be delivered within the constraint—the budget. This modifies the CPPRRSS model as shown in Figure 4.4.

Risk management will be mainly focused on events that might affect the budget. For DPP, benefit-risk and cost-risks had to be weighed together: "How do we make sure the target population can access the finance products without high-cost advertising or setting up help centers?"

For St Edburg's the risks were about rework and unanticipated repairs creating unplanned cost: "Will we find that the footings need fixing when we take the wall down?"

The decisions and actions taken are conditioned by the impact on the remaining budget and different levels of reserves available. They are not necessarily the best possible decision or action, but the best allowed by the constraint.

Developing the Budget-Planning in Uncertainty

Absolute cost-constrained projects such as St Edburg's are relatively rare in commercial environments. Much more common is the situation where a budgetary constraint is applied too early in the project lifecycle creating nugatory planning actions and generating unnecessary governance interventions as the costs escalate. Many project managers feel this pressure, observing, "If we mention a price or a date, then that immediately becomes the budget and the end-date." In project language, the governance group was converting single figure estimates into constraints.

Given a single figure as an estimate, the best a sponsor or stakeholder can do is say it is "too high," or maybe "sounds about right," or "I'll go with that." All pretty unhelpful responses. Consider the difference when the stakeholder is presented with an estimate as a range. The conversation goes more like this. Project manager: "The costs lie between $15,000 and $20,000, and I think, given what we currently know, it is likely to be nearer $20,000." Stakeholders: "Why such a big range?," "Why are you not more certain?," "How can I agree to that? What do we need to know before committing?"

This is a much healthier, much more constructive interaction. There is even a chance that the stakeholders will become engaged in the process.

The appropriate result of a conversation about cost-estimates between the sponsor and the project manager is an understanding about the significance of the difference between the project manager's cost estimate and the sponsor's budgetary limit (cost constraint). A good estimate must:

- Appropriately reflect the level of uncertainty
- Identify the drivers of uncertainty
- Reflect current experience based on history and trends

…while setting a constraint is merely a condition for the success of the project.

Presenting Uncertainty

So how can you avoid the trap set where the stakeholder won't engage and insists on a single value estimate, which they will then hang you by?

This was the situation at Philby. Philby is a company supplying the construction industry with materials. It has a headquarters and some small offices/outlets around the country. Their practice when investing in internal IT projects was to set up fixed price contracts with suppliers, with severe penalty clauses for cost overruns and for failure to deliver the required outcomes. Suppliers were made aware of these conditions during the tendering process.

A Board-level decision was taken to upgrade the hardware and software platforms used by all management and administration staff in the company. The business case specifically recognized that the value from this investment would only be gained if all the managers and staff were made competent in the use of the new capabilities of the kit. This meant that the project would need to be responsible for the training too.

When estimating for planning purposes, the fundamental concern is to ensure that the inherent uncertainty due to the relative uniqueness of the product or the approach is understood and addressed. In this project, as with most projects, during the early stages, there was little detailed information on what the outputs would be, how many there would be, and in some cases how they would be created. In this situation, ranged estimates are necessary to reflect the levels of uncertainty. As time passed more knowledge was gained, the ranges were revised, becoming narrower, indicating higher confidence levels.

Table 4.3 shows an extract of an estimate from one of the bidders for the implementation of Philby's new IT infrastructure. It does use a ranged approach based upon a two-point cost estimate: optimistic (low) and pessimistic (high).

Having a range is good, but the table is a confusing array of numerical data. Some may like it, but most managers would skip read it. Our project managers tell us that when presented with tables like this, many senior managers/sponsors move straight to the bottom line and ask, "Well, what

Table 4.3 An estimation table

Products	Number required		Unit cost		Totals	
	Low	High	Low	High	Low	High
Licensing costs	2,400	2,400	$50	$50	$120,000	$120,000
Hardware upgrades	400	550	$1,200	$1,200	$480,000	$660,000
Dept. servers	5	7	$1,600	$4,000	$8,000	$28,000
Training-operators	5	7	$400	$800	$2,000	$5,600
Training-staff	2,000	2,400	$300	$1,000	$600,000	$2,400,000
					$1,210,000	$3,213,600

is it, $1.2M or $3.2M?" (Sponsors usually round down!). The lack of precision (they want a single figure) is seen as poor management (poor estimating ability) on the part of the project manager. So less experienced project managers hide the uncertainty—because they confuse it with their own uncertainty—and the spiral into obfuscation and poor budgetary practices has begun.

If you focus on the last two columns, the meat of the table is there in a clear and emphatic way. There is no uncertainty about licensing costs, and apart from 'Training-staff' the variances are numerically driven, that is the value is dependent on the number of components affected and so are, in essence, controllable and contained. The 'big ticket' item, 'Training-staff' is different. We have no idea, nor any evidence as to how to control this cost. So, perhaps a sensible option here is to buy a little knowledge, maybe run an investigation.

A problem with two-point estimates is that it encourages an approach that has been heavily criticized, but which, nevertheless, remains common, and that is to take an average and use that as the constraint value. What are the implications for taking a mid-point as the 'planned value' (PV)? Have a look at Figure 4.5. Even if the estimate—the range—follows a normal distribution, which is unlikely (most estimates have a skewed distribution), taking the midpoint, the 'most likely' (ML) value, means that 50 percent of the time the project will come in above that budget figure. Does the project manager or the sponsor really want only a one in two chance of coming in on or under budget? Sounds like a poor bet if your reputation is riding on it.

$$PV = \frac{O+(4*ML)+P}{6}$$

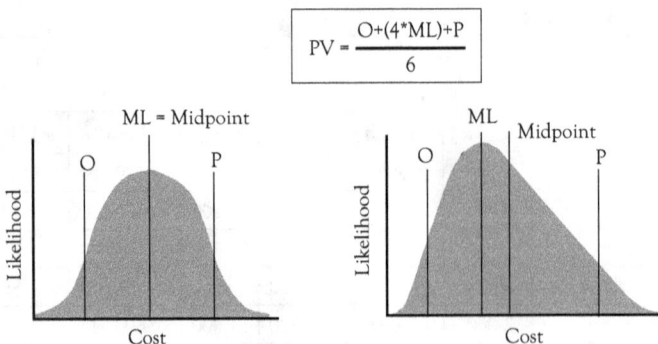

Figure 4.5 Plotting an estimate

The situation is even worse, of course, if the distribution is skewed as the 'most likely' point (ML) in this circumstance is often a lot less than 50 percent of the total possible values. When the distribution is skewed, the mode and the mean do not lie neatly together.

Barry Boehm (1981) in his early work on software cost estimation presented the case against taking the midpoint and argued for a third value—the planning value upon which to base your plan. He used this to develop his cone of uncertainty model (Figure 4.6), with the 'cost at completion' being the planning value.

The cone of uncertainty describes the reduction of the amount of uncertainty during the life of a project and reflects what every experienced project manager knows intuitively. The later you wait to confirm the budgetary figure the more likely you are to be right. In fact, unlike risk where there are five risk strategies, to manage budget uncertainty there are only three: buy information, make assumptions, or wait.

Boehm suggests that it is perfectly reasonable for a range of uncertainty to be as wide as +400 percent and –25 percent during the early stages of a project. (Most project managers are not that brave.) The asymmetry is explained by an effect called estimating-optimism bias. As commented by Steve McConnell (2006) in his comprehensive book on Software Estimation:

Considering that optimism is a near-universal fact of human nature,
software estimates are somewhat undermined by what I think of as

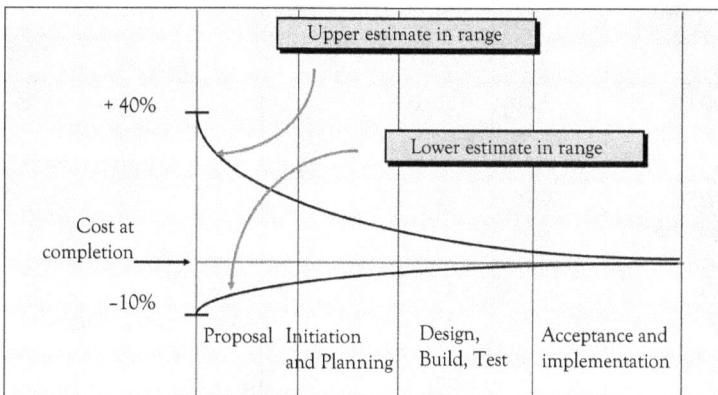

Figure 4.6 The cone of uncertainty

a Collusion of Optimists. Developers present estimates that are opti-mistic. Executives like them because they imply that desirable business targets are achievable. Managers like them because they show support for upper managements' objectives. And so the software project is off and running with no one ever taking a critical look at whether the estimates were well founded.

Let's get back to Philby's project. Another supplier had a highly experienced project manager respond to the tender. She was aware of the procurement rules and the sensitivity of the company to cost over-runs. She realized that by including the training, Philby's had turned the engagement from a simple, low-risk rollout, to a more complex project. She also understood that she needed to engage the stakeholders in the right conversation—one that focused on the essential drivers of uncer-tainty. So, she developed the estimation table shown in Table 4.4.

Firstly, her presentation was much less 'noisy.' She had only displayed the information the stakeholders needed to help focus their thinking. The table showed the sources and significance of the uncertainty in the

Table 4.4 *Presenting an estimate and the sources of uncertainty*

Products	Totals		% variance line item	% variance budget	Uncertainty source
	Low	High			
Licensing costs	$120,000	$120,000	0%	0%	None: fixed price
Hardware upgrades	$480,000	$660,000	38%	5%	Number of upgrades needed uncertain
Dept. servers	$8,000	$28,000	250%	1%	No agreement from Depts. on server upgrades
Training-operators	$2,000	$5,600	80%	0%	Unsure of the amount of training time
Training-staff	$600,000	$2,400,000	317%	57%	No agreement on training approach or how long it will take
	$1,210,000	$3,213,600			

estimation of costs for the project. The first thing to notice is that not all of the costs listed are estimates. For example, 'Licensing costs' are a fixed price and are entirely certain. This is important as it affects how the management reserve—how unknown-unknowns are dealt with. If the costing model is a mixture of fixed-price items and estimates, is it appropriate to apply a contingency charge to the whole amount? Should you not perhaps exclude the fixed-price items?

The real value of this table was of course that with the sources of uncertainty highlighted she could now have a genuine debate:

1. Software costs: Why this supplier? Are you sure they provide the best deal?
2. Hardware upgrades: Should we spend time establishing the exact number of systems that need upgrading before confirming the budget? A simple inventory question.
3. Dept. servers: What can the steering group members do to reduce the uncertainty around participation by recalcitrant departments?
4. Training-operators: Should we dry run the training to find out how much time the training will take?
5. Training staff: What approach is preferred for the training? Who will decide this? Should the project be initiated until this issue is resolved given the centrality of the competency requirement in the business case?

The most ingenious device she used was the '% variance budget column.' No manager could overlook the fact that there was little point worrying about anything else if the 'Training-staff' issue was not resolved.

Her company's bid won the contract—and no penalties were incurred. It was planned using the CPPRRSS model with the products (outputs) estimated in terms of numbers and size in narrowly defined ranges and costed processes tightly associated with each output, including the training approach.

She used one other important planning approach. One that is particularly sensible when cost is the primary constraint. With her need to stay within budget, and knowing the importance of the effectiveness of the training to the project success, the project manager knew this was not the time to adopt innovative solutions. Neither she, nor Philby's, or indeed anyone she knew had previous experience of eLearning. She decided she would leave that as an opportunity for someone else on another project!

Drawing Upon Past Data

A few years back one of our MSc students focused her dissertation on the use of lessons learned in the planning of projects. She was working in the retail sector, and her initial findings were promising. In the presence of a strong central project office, almost 98 percent of projects, over a three-year period, had a documented lessons learned report approved and filed by the relevant governance group. However, then the research faltered. There was incontrovertible evidence that these reports had *never* been accessed by subsequent projects. Even the evidence of informal communication of learning from previous projects was at best circumstantial, more dependent upon the personalities involved than the process adopted.

The results were discussed with the project office manager, who was understandably disappointed. The actions they took as a consequence of this study are still in place today and are now an integral element of every project planned there. When the motivation for a project is presented, it must demonstrate that it can answer this question: "What previous or currently running project is this project similar to?" The project motivation documentation must show evidence that the experience gained by these projects, and any associated learning, has been taken into account. The critical questions from a budget perspective are:

- What was the initial and final budget?
- What factors influenced the final budget figure?
- How is this new project different?

The project manager when developing the plan and costing for the Philby's project had drawn up a table in support of her estimates (Table 4.5). This highlighted the extent of previous experience of carrying out this type of activity in Philby's and similar organizations. It makes clear to the steering group why the eLearning option estimating value correctly has such a wide range.

Table 4.5 Identifying the impact of previous experience on estimating

Products	Totals		Experience
	Low	High	
1. Licensing costs	$120,000	$120,000	Strategic supplier
2. Hardware upgrades	$480,000	$660,000	Twice in last 5 years
3. Dept. servers	$8,000	$28,000	Twice in last 5 years
4. Training–operators	$2,000	$5,600	Twice in last 5 years
5. Training–staff	$600,000	$2,400,000	Face-to-face training twice in the last five years Never set up online training before
	$1,210,000	$3,213,600	

Introducing the Budget Cube

So how did she go about developing the total budget? A budget is not a number. It is a set of 'line items,' each associated with a cost. When developing the budget, particularly during the early stages when the level of uncertainty is high, it can be helpful to use a budget cube that integrates three perspectives:

- Organizational breakdown structure (OBS): The sources of resource for the project;
- Product breakdown structure (PBS): The set of products to be delivered by the project;
- Cost breakdown structure (CBS): The categories of cost over the project's life.

Figure 4.7 shows the budget cube. To use it, you consider a 'slice' at a time, either horizontally or vertically and then stack them together. Its value comes from taking these different perspectives, which allows you to cross-validate, to pick up omissions and double counting that a single view might give rise to. It is also progressive in that if you are stalled looking at it one way, approaching from a different tack can unlock your thinking. All good planning tools should allow progress even when there is a lot of missing data.

When specific resource requirements are unclear, the categories of cost probably won't be. Knowledge of the products to be produced suggests

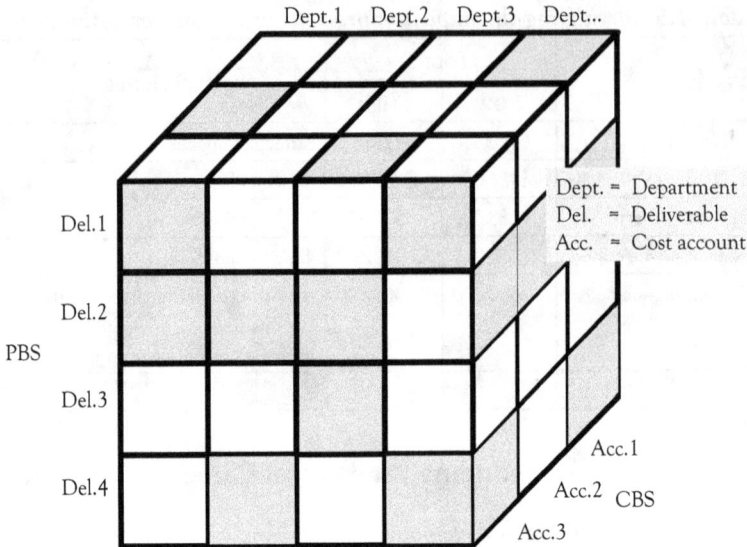

Figure 4.7 The budget cube (Adapted from Turner 2014)

the types of resources, and the types of resources suggest the processes and therefore the categories of cost: labor, management, services, and so on, to consider, and so round we go.

Each perspective gives a different analysis, and each reveals different factors to be taken into consideration in the final budget. Many of the questions require consultation with stakeholders and policymakers; a project manager working alone cannot answer them. For example:

- The CBS identifies the need for an allowance for expenses. These costs can be easily missed if a PBS or resource only view is taken. Should these costs be included in the budget?
- The effort costs associated with implementation are higher in the PBS than the OBS. This is a common problem. The PBS assumes a particular effort for each deliverable produced, but there are often opportunities for savings in time and effort achieved through the rationalization of processes.
- The CBS identifies the potential for increased license fees and the possibility of tax being payable. Are these costs attributable to the budget for this project?

- The CBS distinguishes between costings for internal staff and contractors. Are only direct costs included or are fully burdened costs to be used?
- In the OBS it is clear that there are other parts of the organization that need to be involved in this project, for example procurement and office services. Should their costs be included in the budget?
- The OBS also identifies the time that will be spent by the staff (users) in being trained. Should their time be taken into account in the budget?

As an illustration of the use of the budget cube, let's look at the figures from Philby's project. In Figure 4.8, the initial position shows that the three perspectives give different totals. Which, if any, is correct? By allocating the money by using the combined views of sources of resource and costs, products and costs; and products and sources of resource, a clear picture emerges of what is giving rise to the cost, where omissions have been made, and thus how complete the budget analysis is.

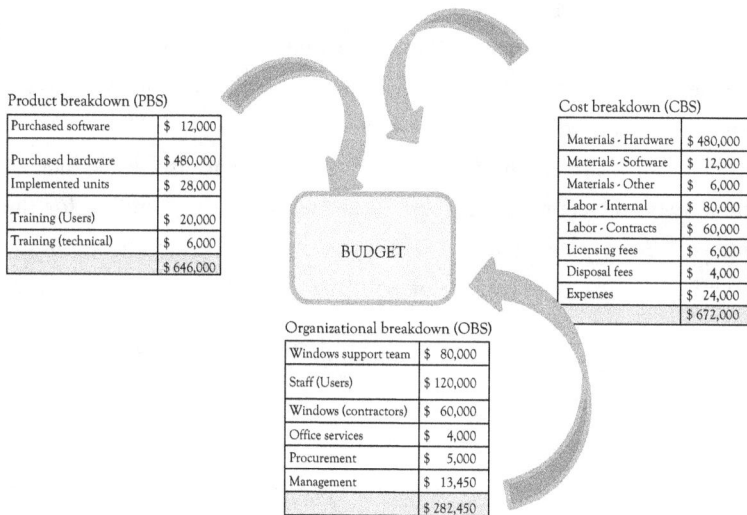

Product breakdown (PBS)

Purchased software	$ 12,000
Purchased hardware	$ 480,000
Implemented units	$ 28,000
Training (Users)	$ 20,000
Training (technical)	$ 6,000
	$ 646,000

Cost breakdown (CBS)

Materials - Hardware	$ 480,000
Materials - Software	$ 12,000
Materials - Other	$ 6,000
Labor - Internal	$ 80,000
Labor - Contracts	$ 60,000
Licensing fees	$ 6,000
Disposal fees	$ 4,000
Expenses	$ 24,000
	$ 672,000

BUDGET

Organizational breakdown (OBS)

Windows support team	$ 80,000
Staff (Users)	$ 120,000
Windows (contractors)	$ 60,000
Office services	$ 4,000
Procurement	$ 5,000
Management	$ 13,450
	$ 282,450

Figure 4.8 Constructing the budget for Philby's IT project

Budgets for Control Versus Budgets for Planning

Table 4.6 shows the impact of various incentivization types on contractual behavior, specifically how often the project delivered within the budget. It supports the view that where a fixed-price or target-cost budget is agreed with a supplier, projects are less likely to overrun in terms of cost. When the incentivization is based on outcomes or activities (final-outcome and cost-plus-fees), the chance of coming in on budget is severely diminished—with around 80 percent of contracts examined being over budget.

It's no surprise that in contractual situations the budget is acting both as an agreement and as a way of setting the supplier goals. What is less certain is whether using this device to motivate project managers is as appropriate. When investigating how end-dates were set on projects (see 'What do we mean by end-date?' in Chapter 2) we found that artificially imposing a constraint rarely achieved its purpose, especially when issues remained unresolved, and often led to more stress and anxiety rather than improved performance within the project.

This effect of applying a constraint as a motivator has been analyzed on a number of occasions in the case of setting budgets. Two identical projects run by different project managers were set up, one with a budget of $1,000 and the other at $750. When completed, the actual expenditure was as shown in Table 4.7.

Which is the better result? Project 1 because it delivered under budget? Or perhaps Project 2 because it delivered the same solution as Project 1 but at a lower cost? Or, is this the wrong question?

We ran a survey on a few project managers and asked: "Which of these two budgets would be best to use when seeking funding for the project?" And, "Which budget would you use to bring out the best in the team?" We're sure you got the answers: to the first question, the answer

Table 4.6 Impact of incentivization on budget performance

	Fixed-price	Target-cost	Payment based on final-outcome	Cost-plus-fee
Under budget	35%	30%	8%	9%
On budget	35%	24%	17%	9%
Over budget	30%	46%	75%	82%

Source: Meng and Gallagher (2012).

Table 4.7 Budget setting exercise

	Expenses	
	Budgeted amount	**Actual results**
Project 1	$1,000	$950
Project 2	$750	$850

Source: Churchill (1984).

was a unanimous vote for Project 1. No one wanted to go back and ask for more. The response to the second question wasn't quite so consistent, but there was a large majority vote for Project 2.

The conclusion to be drawn is that budgets can be used for planning and incentivization, and the best budget for planning may not be the best budget for control. So, it is worthwhile making sure that these two uses do not get confused. We suspect that sponsors do just that. Best practice would be first to understand the planned budget, based upon adequate estimating before you start to get tricky and play around to create a control budget.

How tight you should set this control budget is also an interesting and important question. In some studies, the impact on spending under different regimes has shown that when the budget is regarded as being too tight the net effect is spectacular overspending.

The graph in Figure 4.9 shows the results of this research. When the budget is thought to be fair but tight, cost performance is good; however, when it is regarded as far too tight, cost control is lost. A lesson for many

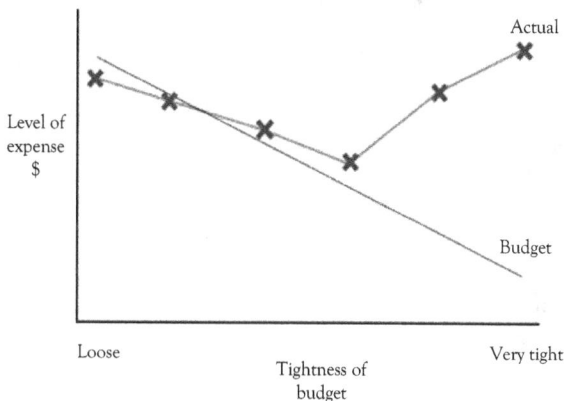

Figure 4.9 Impact over over-tight constraint on overall cost performance

project sponsors to take to heart: and perhaps is why all the effort made in DPP to transparently link the cost cap to the benefit turned out so well.

Reflections

Budgets can be a trial to many project managers; so much admin, and so many hours of tedious work. But, planning a project without a budget is like driving a car with some of the controls missing: scary and a very uncomfortable ride for the passengers.

Brooks (1995) said it all in his seminal text 'The Mythical Man Month':

> *The budget… is not merely a constraint; the budget is one of the managers' most useful documents. The existence of the budget forces technical decisions that otherwise would be voided; and, more important, it forces and clarifies policy and decision.*

Here are some questions you might like to consider:

1. If you do not account for all the costs of your project how is control exercised on those items not included? How does that affect your planning and management?
2. What techniques do you use to handle and convey uncertainty when developing, reviewing, or providing estimates? Could the approaches discussed in the Philby's case be adapted for use in your situation?
3. Have you made use of lessons learned from other projects when planning or discussing your project with stakeholders? Would the deliberate use of comparisons with previous projects help when developing business cases and project plans in your organization?
4. What techniques do you use to develop a project budget? Could the budget cube help when discussing costs with your stakeholders?
5. Do you exercise cost monitoring or cost control? How well would your current approach deal with a tightly cost-constrained project?

CHAPTER 5

When It Really Does Have to Work

There are projects in which some, maybe even most, of the possible outcomes are so threatening that their occurrence cannot be tolerated. Should something go wrong—should it not go to plan—there is no mitigation available. If you are driving a car and the engine malfunctions, it can be annoying, even frightening, but it'll be a whole lot more final if the engine malfunctioning is in a spacecraft!

There are degrees of criticality, ranging from safety-critical performance in a nuclear power station to life-and-death rescue missions, to correct compliance with regulations set out in legislation. In each case, project failure always incurs severe penalties.

In these projects, the avoidance of risk drives the planning. The constraint at the top of the hierarchy is 'quality'—it is total conformance to a pre-specified capability. This forces a modification to the usual planning process. The focus is to avoid the possibility of events occurring that cannot be managed; it is on the use of processes where the known performance indicates very high levels of reliability with no surprises, and inevitably, it is on testing.

The gold standard for testing is verification. Verification is a technique to prove that the processes used are the right processes used in the right way. This is quality assurance, and it ensures that any errors that arise will be known and predictable.

The other approach is testing by validation. This quality control technique compares a product's performance against its predicted performance, but only in those situations that the tester thought of and could find a way to simulate. In practice, this is a risky approach!

Testing—A Possible Solution?

Let's consider this situation. Three months after the national qualification grades were released in the UK there were still several thousand individuals who had not received their results. It was a national scandal, with questions raised by politicians as to whether the body responsible should keep its role.

The problem was caused, as is not unusual, by a newly upgraded IT system. It just didn't work as specified, and it cost the Head of IT his job. The mess was sorted out manually for that year but the next years' results would be ready in a matter of months. It was made quite plain to the new appointee, Sally, that any failures next year could not and would not be tolerated. The CEO was clear that it could be the end of the organization.

So Sally initiated the zero errors no exceptions (ZENO) project. This was not a maintenance project to fix bugs. The primary outcome of the project was to prove to the stakeholders (internal and external) that the poor performance of the system would not, could not, happen again.

It has long been known that coding generates errors at a predictable ratio of total coding. Different languages and different generators have different gearing ratios, but the curve is generic. Clearance rates vary according to the aggressiveness of the testing, but once again, the general shape of the curve remains constant. The one niggling problem is the inability of any validation testing regime to demonstrate zero defects. It only takes one disconfirming instance to show something held to be true is false, while thousands of confirming cases do not prove it. Reality can be so asymmetrical!

The vital management decision, therefore, is when to declare the system 'safe' to go live. Where do you draw the line? What would be acceptable to the ZENO project's stakeholders? How can you know?

The project plan was based on two models: the defects removal curve and a V-development model.

The defect removal curve model, shown in Figure 5.1, requires that test cases are generated in numbers and designed to challenge the logic, and test the input and the output flows identified by the requirements. Good tests are those that identify a defect; poor tests are those that do not—an interesting inversion for some practitioners. And everything is

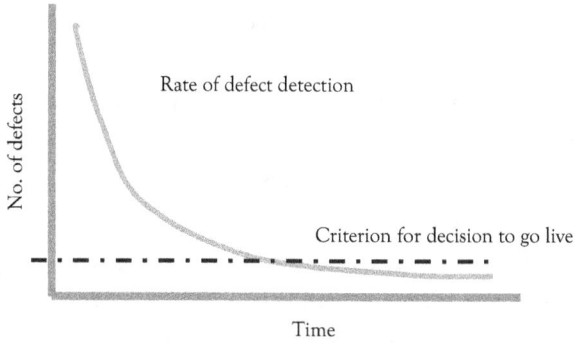

Figure 5.1 Idealized defect removal curve

measured: type of defect, severity, location, and rate. In the final analysis, it is the rate that matters. When the rate dips below and stays below an agreed rate the product is ready for release to the next stage.

Sally combined the defect removal curve with a V-model for determining when tests should be created. In the waterfall model of product development, testing and test cases are created late in the product life cycle, after the design and development stages are complete. It seems natural to batch the work up this way as the appropriate resources are available. In the V-model, however, the sequence and the way resources are engaged changes—the planning is different. While development activities follow the V down and up, test creation—and some of the testing—doesn't. It goes across, as shown in Figure 5.2.

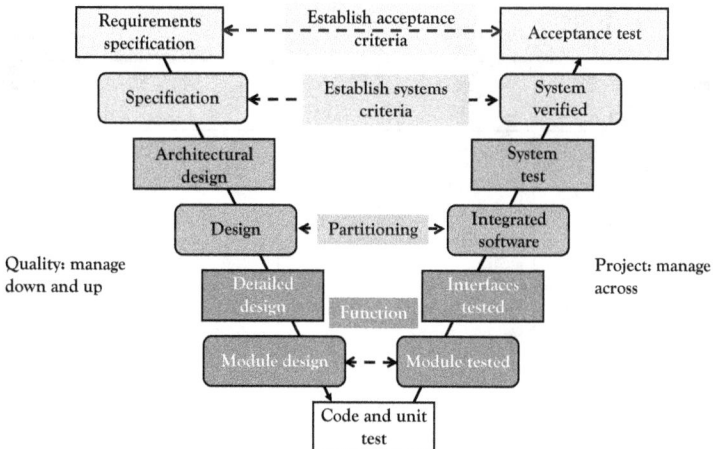

Figure 5.2 The V-development model

This approach meant that the project had to regress the product all the way back to the original requirements. It will come as no surprise to those working in IT that finding these requirements was not as easy as it ought to have been. Additionally, in a year, the user requirements had morphed—what was considered as 'good performance' had changed. Perhaps the most critical success factor for the ZENO project was persuading the internal stakeholders that testing was not simply a technical problem. They would be part of the solution.

The way tests were constructed and approved was also new to the organization. 'Use cases' are common analytical tools nowadays and they are a good way of making the process of identifying requirements and business rules 'real' to the user community. What is less common is to combine them with developing detailed test criteria at the same time. This was done using Gilb and Finzi's (1988) 'clear-the-fog-from-the-target' principle. They assert that: "All critical attributes can be specified in measurable, testable terms, and the worst-acceptable level can be identified." Table 5.1 illustrates how this was applied in the ZENO designs.

Each critical capability was documented, and the measurable performance criteria agreed with the users. Following the Gilb and Finzi (1988) approach, the project split tests into two types. Tests that proved that a capability was present or not—that is giving a simple binary outcome were called 'functional requirements.' When tests were designed to

Table 5.1 A non-functional requirement

Effective	Scale	Test	Planned value	Currently	Standard value	Risk
Accurate	%	% age filled forms correctly processed from the test population	99%	84%	84%	H
Independent	Time	Hours to solo operation	5 hours	1.5 days	2 hours	L
Efficient	Count	Number of filled forms processed in one hour from the test population	9	5	9	M

find out 'how much' of a capability was present, these were identified as 'non-functional requirements (NFRs).'

Suppose a system should provide the capability to divide two numbers. A simple test can demonstrate conformance to this requirement. But, for most users, it is how accurately, how quickly, and perhaps how easy it is to use the division function, that matters. These three are all NFRs. Determining precisely what is wanted when scalable terms like accuracy, speed, and ease of use are being tested is achieved by defining them solely and entirely by a set of tests and agreed results.

The names of the attributes are just labels. So, in the example in Table 5.1, what the NFR 'effective' means isn't that someone is 'accurate, independent, and efficient.' It exactly means that someone is 'effective' when he or she can achieve the planned results for all of the three tests set out in the table.

The impact of using what was a testing schedule as the basis for defining the work packages and the sequencing and pacing of the work in the ZENO project was profound. Tasks were sized, based on the tests and severity of test values defined by the users. The pace of work, identifying when the next work package could be opened by a resource, was determined by the clearance rate of defects.

After four months of focused testing the defect curves for the various capabilities of the system and of the system as a whole all fell below the 'accept' line and Sally used this to gain agreement to put the system live.

The company is still there, with its reputation restored: as is Sally!

Process Conformance—the Only Solution

There are situations and projects where quality control on its own is not an option.

The need was to decommission a Magnox nuclear power station site. Safety was of paramount importance: for the owners, the project team, the contractors, and the public. It was set up as a project—there was a budget, and there was an end date; with a schedule of work, a sponsor, and all the other trappings. The various tasks, activities, and processes were set out in considerable detail—and strictly following the procedure was the only rule. It was only by following due process that it could be proved that all known possible risks had been addressed.

So when it became apparent, as work progressed, that neither the budget nor the end date was even remotely feasible, there was no contest; no wringing of hands. The project charged straight through these 'constraints,' because in that hierarchy staying safe was the only thing that mattered. In that regard, the project was planned and run more like a continuous operation than a bounded piece of work. The fundamental approach adopted was to use a verification process to prove safe conduct. In such a circumstance, 'process is king.'

Planning—the Only Way Out

In July 2018, the world held its breath as a skilled team fought to bring 12 boys and their coach out of a water-drowned cave. A documentary setting out the planning and approach can be found by scanning this QR code (Figure 5.3), or by typing the URL shown into a browser. It is on YouTube.

The planning is a perfect example of the planning approach when there is only one acceptable outcome for a project. That outcome wasn't, by the way, that there would be no fatalities. Firstly, there was a fatality, the tragic loss of the brave Thai SEAL. Secondly, and this is abundantly clear in the documentary, all of the planning was done under the acceptance that there was likely to be casualties among the rescued. However, and this is also clear, the condition that *had* to be met by the planning was that no deaths would be caused by the process of extraction.

Let's look at the planning and why it was carried out the way it was.

First, there are no standard processes or work practices to implement. So, it's not like the Magnox problem. The crucial planning decision was

https://youtu.be/-esjQLvsgTs

Figure 5.3 Cave rescue YouTube documentary

to get world experts in this specialist field of cave diving rescue and to ensure that the tasks were allocated to the most suitable expert.

Second, there were risks that they could not handle. One of them was if a boy panicked while being shepherded out in the very frightening conditions. No management action guaranteed a good result. This meant that a way had to be found that eliminated the possible event called 'boy panics.' The strategy adopted of avoiding the risk event led to a solution in which the boys were sedated. This, in turn, required that an innovative solution is found: how to move sedated bodies safely while submerged and in the pitch black?

The third observation is that having found a potential solution—a five-point attachment facemask, and a carrying strap—the approach was tested repeatedly with volunteers in a swimming pool. The planning had triggered a sandbox moment, no improvising! And the introduction of this solution underpinned much of the rest of the planning. The critical risk translated to making sure that the precious mask was *never* accidentally dislodged throughout the transit because that would break the constraint: no deaths caused by the extraction.

It is well worth watching the short film as it is an example of courage, humans at their best, and a tour de force in project management planning where failure is not an option under challenging circumstances.

The Role of Risk in Planning

As we so often have to repeat when teaching risks in our workshops, risk management is not a back-covering exercise. We do not create long lists of risks so when the problem arises the project manager can respond with "I told you so!" If a risk is on the risk log it means you have chosen to do something about it; and that means costs, time and management attention. As we see in the Project Mission Model™, risks contribute to our understanding of the scope of the project—what deliverables and activities we must include. So, when you agree with the client or other stakeholders that a risk should be included on the log, you are agreeing as to what risk strategy, and what set of management actions have a place in the plan.

The normal way of dealing with risk financially is through the allocation of contingency—a budgetary allowance for the known-unknowns—Chapter 4 on budgeting describes this in more detail. In our workshops, project managers complain that while they may highlight risks to stakeholders, the next natural step of making allowances for them in the scope, budget, or schedule is blocked. It turns out; nobody likes paying up front to prevent or reduce the probability of something that *might* happen. It seems to rankle in the mind of some operational managers who would rather wait and see if it happens, and if it does, then… No wonder projects can find themselves 'up the creek without a paddle!'

In end-date and cost-constrained projects described in Chapters 3 and 4, the 'wait until it happens' approach is untenable, but, in mission-critical projects, it can result in, literally, death. The infeasibility of fix-on-failure in mission-critical projects justifies and forces the special approach to planning required. What might appear as a contingency and therefore optional in other projects is in this type of project fully incorporated in the budget. In mission-critical projects, the level of contingency set aside will either be considerably less or zero.

Planning When the Tolerance of Risk Is Low

When the top constraint is the need for a specific capability to be provably present, whether it is a student awards system, a decommissioned nuclear power plant, or 12 boys and their coach safe, then making trade-offs is almost always inappropriate.

In each of the stories in this chapter, the project had to find solutions that addressed critical risks: risks *so perilous* that it was better to consider them as CSFs. Each project had to achieve an outcome without fail, or it would be a failure, a concept closely aligned with a CSF.

The three project managers worked closely with SMEs, sometimes world experts, to understand the nature of the risks and to develop acceptable project strategies. (The term 'acceptable' is defined solely in terms of the degree to which the actions reduce the probability, or the impact, of the risk.) In the three projects, the principal constraint *is* that failure is not an option and that influences the CPPRRSS process (Figure 5.4). The planning sequence is a tightly coupled iteration between risks and

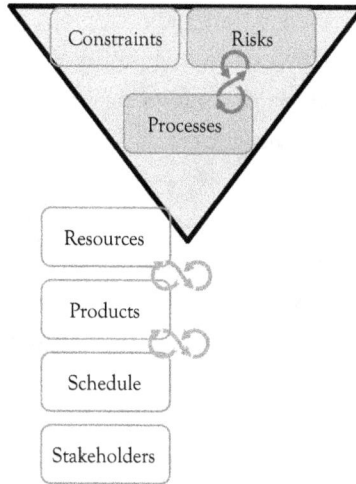

Figure 5.4 Planning steps for mission-critical projects

processes. And process is king. Innovation, if accepted at all, is kept in a sandbox until it has been proved, and only used if essential to the completion of the project. Project management in these types of projects is perhaps more than in any other, an exercise in a disciplined approach.

Project Management When the Tolerance of Risk Is Low

The real professional is one who knows the risks, their degree, their causes, and the action necessary to counter them, and shares this knowledge with his colleagues and clients. (Gilb and Finzi 1988).

Much of our work on the development of organizational and personal project management capability over the last 25 years was fueled by research we undertook on behalf of CSC—the giant US computer company—in 1989. The problems facing us were "Why is project performance so unpredictable?" and "When running projects that are mission-critical, are there special people that should be assigned as the project manager?"

Research conducted on some of CITI's data at the University of Limerick (Leonard and Willis 2000) investigated whether domain specialism was valuable in high performing projects managers. The results are interesting. They found that when projects were complex and driven by general constraints such as time and cost, projects were more likely to be successful when run by experienced project managers rather than by SMEs. So the prejudice which leads to suggesting that all engineering projects being better run by engineers; all IT projects being better run by IT specialists, is ill-founded.

However, when the constraints are related to the content of the project, the weight of evidence supports the proposition that the project is better run by SMEs with project management understanding. The mission-critical planning discussed here gives us some insights into why this might be:

- In all three projects, the project manager drew upon very specialist expertise—in the case of the cave rescue, the best expert in the world. As stated in the documentary, "You don't make your best cave diver the leader of the project—they need to be in the cave" But, the project leader, the US Captain, had extensive experience of diving and had been involved in cave rescue situations. This meant he was able to command the respect of all of the team players, and he could evaluate and prioritize the input from his team. In these situations, whose voice should be listened to is a critical judgment, and that takes subject matter expertise.
- "This is the way it is going to be." At some point on these projects, the project manager has to take on the responsibility for the decision: 'it is going to be this way.' In the case of the ZENO project, Sally had to convince the Board and many other stakeholders that they were going to have to do something they felt had already been done, but that this time it would work. Her position as an expert in the field of software development and testing was crucial to deciding on the approach, and in being able to convince others.
- In projects like the Magnox decommissioning, the weight of decision making is against innovation. Only use tried and tested processes, and if none is available, then the deployment of any new means is going to be a very cautious endeavor. There is 'no learn on the job.' As we see in the cave rescue,

even something as simple as carrying the boys was repeatedly trialed in a swimming pool before the rescue. This caution is a characteristic of SMEs. Their very expertise is built on a disciplined approach and a value system that respects the prior experience and proven procedures used by their fellow professionals.

Reflections

With any luck, you will never have to run a mission-critical project, but there are aspects of the approach to their management that are worth considering when planning your projects. For example:

1. Do others consider you primarily a domain (technical) expert or a project manager?
2. In what ways do you think this affects the way you approach planning and executing your project?
3. Do you find that you are routinely adopting 'make good' (i.e., fix-on-failure) as the favored risk strategy?
4. What do you do to gain acceptance for strategies such as risk reduction (paying ahead of time to reduce the likelihood of an event) and risk protection (paying ahead of time to reduce the impact should it happen)?
5. Have you found yourself discouraging innovative approaches when planning and executing a project? Can you explain why?
6. How do you go about getting your stakeholders and requirement givers to clarify what their acceptance criteria are for the capabilities your project has to deliver?

CHAPTER 6

When Stakeholders Really Matter

More and more organizations are using projects to achieve their goals. As discussed in Chapter 1 there has been a shift in emphasis on what makes a project successful. Nowadays it is much more about having the right impact, creating value, and realizing sustainable value, which means paying attention to factors that are far removed from just making the appropriate allocation of resources to well-defined tasks. The focus on outcomes rather than on the delivery of outputs is achieved by attending to the combination of CSFs and constraints.

This may account for why, and to our mind very belatedly, the project management community has woken up to the importance placed on satisfying stakeholders, and the need to ensure that the outputs from a project are adopted and used. It is only as recently as 2013 that the various bodies of knowledge (PMBOK and APM BOK) even recognized the significance of stakeholder engagement as part of the project managers' armory. The project manager can no longer be confident of success by following a technically well-executed schedule. They are dependent on others, collaborating with stakeholders, working with the sponsor, making sure that what the project does deliver is made valuable in the context of the business. You can no longer succeed alone!

Given this re-alignment of management attention, how does the planning process respond? Rather than just ask, 'How much can I spend?,' 'How long have I got?,' and 'What do you want?' The questions need a little more sophistication to surface the satisfaction criteria. Perhaps questions like these:

- *What does success look like?* A surprisingly difficult question to answer for some sponsors—but persevere—because if they don't know, it is unlikely *you* will come up with the right answer.

- *How do you know when the project is completed?* Stopping the project just because you've reached the end-date is rarely a successful ploy, so how do you know when enough is enough? This is fundamental planning information.

- *How will the project be measured/judged?* This is a curiously overlooked question. People respond to what is being measured. In a study repeated many times, a research group deliberately let slip they were recording the number of smiles seen in a library. Without any further communication, the number of smiles rose and stayed high until the group left. The incidence of smiles gradually returned to its original level. (This was known because, of course, the researchers hadn't gone, they just became secretive!) Whatever the project is thought to be measured on, will be the factor that gets most management attention.

Success factors for a project set out those things that we must focus on in our planning and delivery. CSFs are, as their name implies, not important, they are critical—that is they are concerns that should they not be achieved, the project will be seen to have failed. In this way, they are similar to constraints. The project client defines and owns the CSFs, and the project must be planned and delivered to ensure their achievement. However, they can be difficult to tease out from stakeholders.

Clients will often lead you to believe it is all about the money, or it is all about the end-date, but when close attention is paid to the decisions made, it becomes clear that other factors—the critical success factors—are the ones that really dictate their choices and their reactions of disappointment or delight.

A project that demonstrates this point was the construction of the Scottish Parliament Building. This was funded by taxpayers' money and had a widely debated and publicized budget and end-date. It was delivered three years late—twice the original three-year estimate. It was 1,000 percent over budget—the original estimate was between £10m to £40m, and yet the actual cost was £414m.

Why? How? A review of every decision taken by the stakeholders made it quite clear, when it came to making choices, they were much more interested in making a prestige building with high aesthetic values, with spring water flushing the toilets, than staying within budget or finishing on schedule. This was the real CSF—the real constraint—not the money and not the time.

Characterizing Stakeholder-Intensive Projects

This chapter looks specifically at how planning changes on stakeholder-sensitive and stakeholder-led projects. In these types of projects, the fundamental driver for success, the critical success factors, are the way in which the stakeholders behave. If you are on a project where the most important outcome is positive engagement by groups of stakeholders, where the project can only succeed if the stakeholders allow it to, then you are involved in a stakeholder-sensitive project. If you are on a project (or more likely a program) where what you deliver, and how, is dictated by the agendas of influential external stakeholders, then you may be managing a stakeholder-led project.

Role and Agenda-Based Stakeholders

In planning for stakeholder-intensive projects, we suggest you first distinguish between those stakeholders that are involved with your project because of their role; what we term role-based stakeholders and those whose interest and involvement arises from specific agendas they hold: agenda-based stakeholders (Worsley 2016).

Role-Based Stakeholders

Role-based stakeholders are those who have a specific responsibility in the project environment. These are identified during the planning stages as:

- *Governance stakeholders*: individuals and groups who are involved in authorization or approval decisions for the project, for example, sponsor, steering group, and so on.

- *Internal stakeholders*: some individuals and groups internal to the project may be best treated as role-based stakeholders. These include those that support the definition of requirements, and the implementation of the products, as well as those responsible for the operational changes, for example, product owners, users, and so on.

For all of these, it will be possible to define a particular role in the project. Where roles are unclear, or there are overlaps, then techniques such as responsibility charting can be useful.

Responsibility charting (often known by the acronym RACI—responsible, accountable, consulted, informed) is a technique used to identify areas where there are process or decision making ambiguities. The aim is to bring out the differences of opinion and resolve them through consultation and debate. Underpinning the approach is the insight that any particular role has three perspectives—what the person thinks the role is, what other people believe the role is, and what the person actually does. It is worth observing that these are often poorly aligned, one with another.

RACI's usefulness is not only in providing a public and straightforward analysis of roles but also in its ability to uncover where there is a tendency to encourage ambiguity—a lack of clarity to hide behind. Communicating the understanding of roles often exposes issues and areas that require further debate. During planning, RACI is particularly useful for ensuring governance clarity—who can make what decisions about what and when; and for activity clarity—who takes responsibility for doing what and when. An example of a partial RACI can be seen in Table 6.1.

Agenda-Based Stakeholders

Agenda-based stakeholders are those who have an opinion on the project and its conduct and have the power and opportunity to influence it. The identification of agenda-based stakeholders requires an external perspective and demands anticipating who might have an interest through the life of the project and beyond.

In projects where agenda-based stakeholders abound, it is unlikely that the project manager will be well-positioned to understand all of the

Table 6.1 A RACI table

	Project manager	Steering group	Sponsor	Business owner
Develops the business case	R	C	A	R
Approves stage completions	R	C	A/R	C
Resolves cross-functional issues	R	A	I	I
Makes go/no-go decisions		C	A	
Ensures claimed savings are made			A/R	R
Ensures resources are committed	R	A		R
Approves funding and funding changes		A	R	

possible players. The tools to use during the planning stages include techniques such as power and influence mapping, stakeholder checklists, and salience analysis, as well as others (Worsley 2016).

Different approaches and techniques are necessary when planning for role-based stakeholders from those used in analyzing agenda-based groups. Too often, we see the same techniques used for both. As an example, one of the most frequently used tools is the 'power-interest' grid on to which stakeholders are mapped. This is a technique for dealing with agenda-based stakeholders, and not particularly suitable for role-based ones. Consider this: Are you *sure* your sponsor is the most motivated stakeholder? Will the sponsor always feature in the 'high-high' box (see Figure 6.1)?

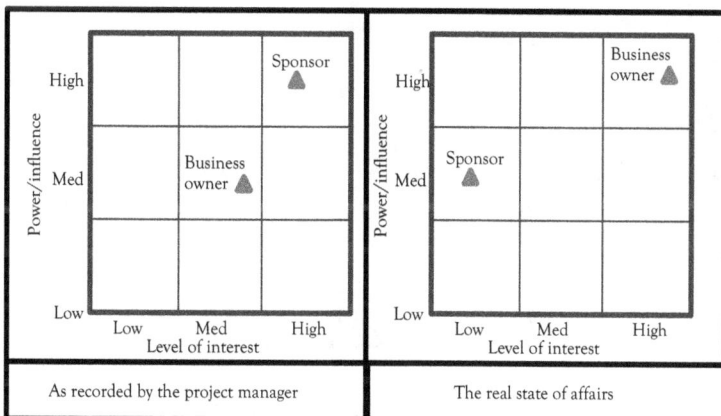

Figure 6.1 Mapping stakeholders on a power-interest grid

Sponsors should be on the grid somewhere. Otherwise, they'd be a poor choice for a sponsor. But many projects suffer because the sponsor is regarded as the most powerful influencer on the project—and it turns out they're not! In the project that Figure 6.1 came from, the project manager had placed the sponsor and the business owner (the operational manager who would inherit the outputs from the project) as shown on the first grid. The actual position was more like the second grid. By misplacing, and therefore mismanaging the stakeholders, the project ended in considerable disarray.

Stakeholder-Neutral to Stakeholder-Led Projects

Of course, every project has at least one stakeholder. Even a project you do for yourself by yourself has you as a stakeholder! It is the number of stakeholders, their positions concerning the project and the nature of their interests and level of power (the mix of role-based and agenda-based stakeholders) that will fundamentally influence the way you can plan and conduct the project.

Figure 6.2 illustrates an approach to classifying projects based on the type and intensity of stakeholder involvement. It is a continuum from

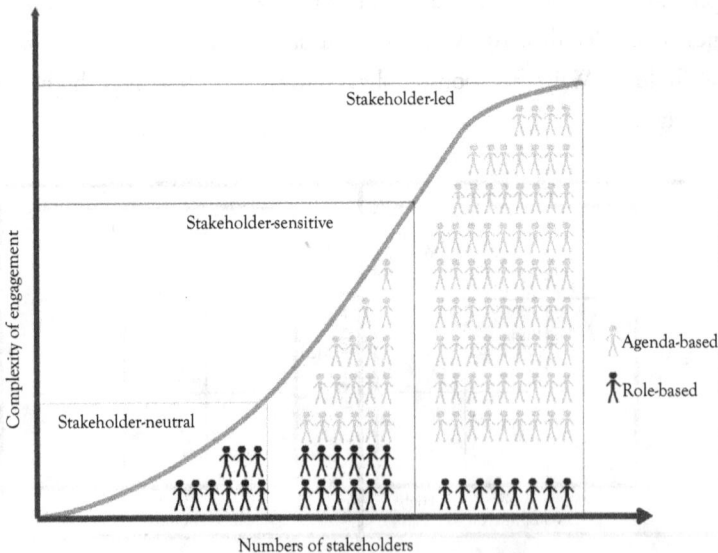

Figure 6.2 *Stakeholders associated with different project types*

stakeholder-neutral to stakeholder-led. Role-based stakeholders dominate stakeholder-neutral projects. Engagement is through governance meetings, simple communications, and training. At the other end of the continuum, stakeholder-led projects involve large numbers of stakeholders, mixed and often conflicting agendas, and are usually in the public domain. These projects demand elaborate engagement plans, and it is the engagement planning itself, which dominates the project planning process.

Let's now have a look at two examples of stakeholder-intensive projects. As you read them, consider:

- Where would you position the two projects on the stakeholder continuum?
- Do you have projects with similar challenges and success factors?
- Can you identify role-based and agenda-based stakeholders in your projects?
- Where do your projects sit on the stakeholder-neutral to stakeholder-led continuum?
- What techniques are you using to analyze and plan stakeholder engagements?

A Case of Super-Sensitive Stakeholder Management

Remploy was a UK government-owned organization offering employment and skills development support for disabled people. Up until 2007, it provided this primarily through its own factories—a network of 83 sites, in every region of the UK. But the world had changed. The thinking among disability groups and leading charities was that for many disabled people working in mainstream employment was much better than in specialized facilities.

There is now an acceptance that disabled people would prefer to work in mainstream employment alongside non-disabled people rather than in sheltered workshops from which they do not progress and develop...
—Remploy's Chief Executive Officer

With the changing dynamics of employment, it was established that for the cost of employing one person in a Remploy factory it could place four people in jobs with mainstream employers.

The early planning showed that 28 factories would need to be closed to meet the financial targets, but the political and social landscape was bleak. Remploy would be terminating posts that had been traditionally safe (protected) job opportunities for the disabled. This was a program no individual, and certainly no politician would find easy to support openly. The project group faced a formidable challenge. They had to convince all those who had an interest that the company had the right approach. This was their critical success factor—what would need to be achieved if the project was to end well:

> *Disability groups, the media, disabled employees and their families, and unions must have confidence in the Remploy approach and believe in its positive effects in the medium to longer term.*

First, Define Your Stakeholder Engagement Approach

The early planning phase was a massive stakeholder engagement exercise. Each of the stakeholder's agendas—groups and individuals—were considered in detail, with named people identified who may be affected by the closure of factories. The stakeholder list consisted of thousands of entries.

The engagement approach and the timing of the engagement were analyzed. Somewhat like a huge soccer game—the planning team had to consider which stakeholders should be on the pitch when they should be brought into play, what positions they should take, and when they could be taken off the field. Timing would be critical—an uncontrolled, untimely invasion of the pitch would be difficult to recover from!

To create appropriate engagement strategies, the planning team had to understand the possibilities for aligning WIIFM ('What's in it for me') factors to improve the success rate of the engagement activities. This, like negotiation processes generally, demanded real out-of-the-box problem-solving thinking. Actions, not directly linked to the final outputs, had to be defined and delivered wholly focused on addressing the stakeholder-related risks.

Political agendas also needed to be managed. That meant looking at all the possible influencing strategies. Who is best placed to influence others, and whom can we influence? As the program director commented,

> *Our job was to give our team the direction, information, and tools to go out and persuade, sometimes cajole but always positively influence the key groups and individuals, then track that it was happening and amend the plan as necessary.*

With jobs at stake, and the complex legislation around the employment of the disabled, careful attention needed to be given to ensuring that due process was carefully followed. It was of great credit to the program that none of the consultations and actions that followed resulted in tribunals or other legal action.

Planning Was Everything

The planning phase took three years, and during this time business-as-usual continued. Why so long? The repercussions of getting it wrong were just so high. Not only was the Remploy business at risk, but also the ability of government and public services to provide real opportunities to some of the most vulnerable people in society would be affected.

Using the insights gained from the stakeholder analysis, the team planned out every single deliverable, every single communication in detail. Scenario planning for each possible interaction was analyzed, and appropriate responses were mapped out. Nothing was left to chance; right the way down to providing the detailed scripts for the meetings and briefings that would be given by the operational line managers.

Retrospective

In the 12 months following this project, Remploy found 6,600 jobs in mainstream employment for people with disabilities—an increase of 27 percent on the previous year and the situation continues to go well. The Remploy modernization program won the Association for Project Managers (APM) Program of the Year Award 2009. This case was originally published in The Project Manager magazine (Worsley 2010).

A Case of Stakeholder-Led Project Management

In 2007, the City of Cape Town started a major transport infrastructure program to introduce the integrated rapid transport (IRT) system. Some of this work continues to this day. The overall aim of the IRT was to bring about a more sustainable and balanced integrated transport system, notably linking the poorer, outlying areas of Cape Town to economic and social nodes in the city.

The first phase focused on the northern suburbs and inner city basin where extreme congestion was regularly experienced during peak traffic periods. A MyCiti bus service was introduced between the Cape Town Civic Centre and the Cape Town International Airport, and for the duration of the hugely successful 2010 FIFA World Cup, the city offered a dedicated MyCiti service to spectators and tourists. Included in the IRT portfolio are the metro rail network, the MyCiti network, conventional bus and minibus operations, metered taxis, and bicycle and pedestrian lanes, all of which are to be eventually connected to make an integrated whole.

Phase 1 IRT was a complex technical challenge. It involved the redevelopment of some of the busiest streets to establish dedicated bus lanes. But this was not the biggest worry for the city. MyCiTi buses, where they were implemented, would compete directly with existing taxi and bus services, and this raised social and public order issues, which could result in a genuine threat to the success of the program. The resistance to the new service was likely to be significant, disruptive, and potentially violent.

A project focusing specifically on the positive engagement of these stakeholders was set up to run in parallel with the construction and operationalization program. This business integration project had one major critical success factor: its implementation was accepted and supported by existing road business, specifically the taxi and bus services.

In Cape Town, taxis are a source of income to large groups of local citizens. A private taxi typically provides a living for at least three families: the driver, the taxi owner, and the franchiser who owns the license to operate in a particular area. Each of these families would be impacted by a change in the competitive environment. Given eight taxi associations, 950 taxis, two bus companies with 200 buses, that is a lot of families.

The taxi associations are managed by powerful community members. They are not averse to aggressive, and sometimes violent, defense of their business interests. These groups continuously fight against what they see as government over-regulation, and there was, at the time, no grounds for a trusted relationship between the various parties involved.

It was clear to the City of Cape Town program team that if they were to be successful in the IRT implementation, integration with the local transport businesses into the new service would be crucial, and that would mean formalizing an informal industry which had resisted regularization for many years.

Planning the Stakeholder Engagement

Early planning activities concentrated on the assessment and analysis of the stakeholder groups involved. In talking with the manager of this project, one message comes through clearly: *If you don't understand your stakeholders' business or understand your stakeholders' agendas, then you are unlikely to find successful solutions to their concerns.* Getting to know the 'players' and creating the appropriate relationships, public and personal, was a major component of this project's activities. This project uses all of the six principles of stakeholder engagement (Figure 6.3).

The project manager was adamant:

> *When we engage with the community we must give them confidence that we are listening and we are reacting to the input they provide us. That means reading back their concerns using 'their voice,' involving them in the development of solutions and being transparent and clear about what we can and cannot achieve.*

The project needed the 'right ears' to hear the real concerns; and the right approaches—those chosen with and by the stakeholders. Without that, the shared development of solutions, which would deliver sustainable relationships with the business community, would never materialize.

This project sought and delivered solutions that just would not have been thought of without this level of engagement in the planning and delivery processes. For example, with the introduction of the IRT, the

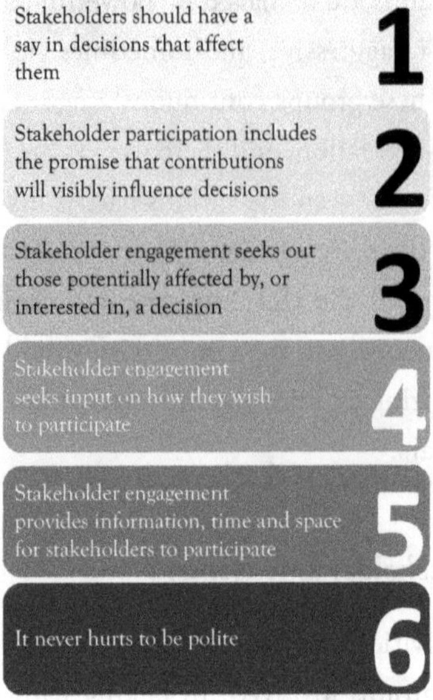

Figure 6.3 The six principles of stakeholder engagement

numbers of passengers available to the taxi operating companies would inevitably go down. In a radical move, the project team proposed a new income scheme based upon the number of kilometers traveled by the taxi rather than the number of passengers. The City Council agreed to back the scheme financially. To achieve this within budget constraints meant reducing the number of taxis on the road, and that meant laying off taxi drivers. To address this, another scheme was set up to provide pension packages for those taxi drivers of or near pensionable age, thus reducing the numbers of drivers and taxis.

Retrospective

The City of Cape Town believed in the critical importance of business community buy-in to the success of the new IRT. They backed this with commitment, resources, and budget. Other cities in South Africa did not take such far-reaching measures. While Cape Town is sometimes criticized for the costs incurred for the IRT development, it is the only city in South Africa that has been able to sustain the new transport system. Others have struggled, often facing aggressive, and sometimes violent, opposition to their metropolitan-regulated schemes.

WHEN STAKEHOLDERS REALLY MATTER   107

In 2012, Cape Town was one of four cities short-listed for the prestigious Sustainable Transport Awards, with its non-motorized transport (NMT) and the bus rapid transit network, MyCiti, receiving an honorable mention. This case study was originally published in Stakeholder-led Project Management: Changing the way we manage projects (Worsley 2016).

Stakeholder-Intensive Project Planning

Both the IRT and Remploy projects are examples of stakeholder-intensive projects. How did you decide to position them on the continuum? Not sure? Consider the critical success factors of the two projects side-by-side:

- *Remploy*: Disability groups, the media, disabled employees and their families, and unions *must have confidence* in the Remploy approach and believe in its positive effects in the longer term.
- *IRT*: Implementation *is accepted and actively supported* by existing road business—specifically the taxi and bus services.

The difference in wording and 'tone' is enough to cause a big difference in planning and execution. Remploy had a solution that was driven by the need to close down existing factories. The purpose of the project planning was to take its agenda-based stakeholders on a shared journey toward these solutions. This is characteristic of a stakeholder-sensitive project.

The IRT program (at least the local business integration part of this program) did not know and could not mandate which solutions could be successful. Stakeholder-led projects, such as these, are game-changers in the way we plan and manage their execution.

Adapting Planning to Stakeholder-Intensity

Stakeholder understanding is an essential part of project initiation and planning. The scope of a project is fundamentally impacted by the size and complexity of the stakeholder landscape. Engagement and communication costs time and money, and stakeholder factors contribute to the project risks. The management of these risks also adds to the scope of, or at least to the contingency for, the project. Yet, communication and engagement are often either under-scoped or simply not included in the scope at all. Communication then becomes 'something we will do *if* we have the time and the money.'

The product breakdown structure (PBS—the outputs required to achieve the outcomes of the project) is the primary tool used for project scoping. Consider your own PBS. Where are the communication and engagement products? Have they been adequately allowed for? How did you go about identifying how much time and effort would be required? In many of the technical projects we looked at, communication either appeared as a single product (called communications) with little evidence of analysis of what this covered or was assumed to be included in the management overhead.

Figure 6.4 is a top-level PBS for a straightforward office move. As a stakeholder-neutral project, the stakeholder engagement is mainly focused on communications and training. These have been included in the scope as 'Training on new telephones' and as a communications product which includes the main pieces of work: 'Launch briefings,' 'Team updates' and a detailed communications plan for the actual move. These are clear in the PBS, and once we have established how many of each product is needed (the number of launch briefings, for example, depends upon how many staff to be briefed); these can be planned into the budget and included in the schedule.

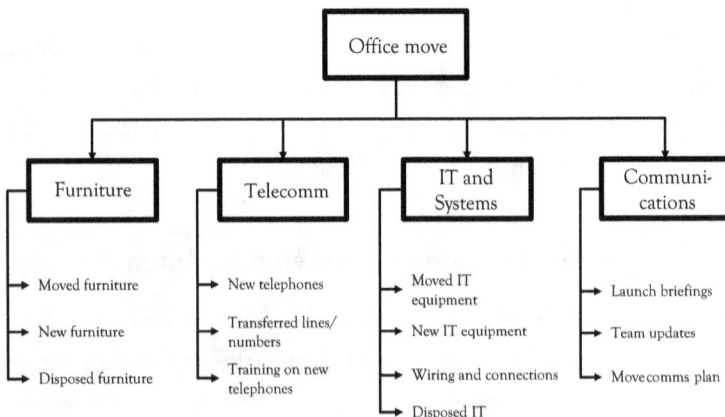

Figure 6.4 **A high-level PBS for an office move**

Now let's look at the PBS for a stakeholder-led project. Figure 6.5 shows an illustrative extract of a PBS for the IRT program. The first thing that should be noticed is that the organizer is quite different. In fact, it looks rather like an organizational breakdown structure. In stakeholder-led projects, the primary driver of scope is the stakeholder groups and the individuals that make them up. In these projects, where the critical success factor is stakeholder-focused (remember the IRT CSF: "taxi and bus services committed to the solution"), the whole purpose of the project is engagement, and that is what defines the scope. This PBS needs further detail, which will come from the identification of stakeholder groupings (how the field of play is to be 'segmented') as well as the analysis of the engagement processes and communication mechanisms to be used.

Stakeholder-sensitive projects sit rather uncomfortably between the two extremes shown in Figures 6.4 and 6.5. If you have ever struggled to structure your PBS; debated where to capture the 'people elements'; weren't sure whether training is its own product or should be positioned along with other delivery elements, then you may well have been dealing with a stakeholder-sensitive project. How you structure the scope does matter, and you were right to struggle with it.

Figure 6.6 (PBS1) is a possible structure for the Remploy project discussed previously. It combines both the approaches already shown with the technical deliverables in their work packages. Within the communications product, the work is structured by stakeholder grouping. For each of these groups, a further breakdown is required of the communication deliverables.

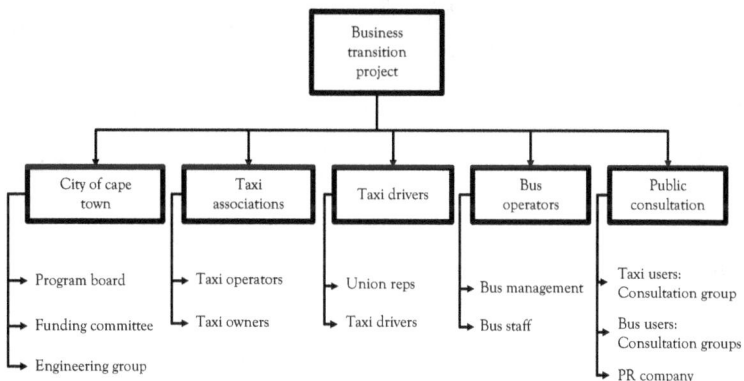

Figure 6.5 A PBS for the IRT program

PBS1

New Remploy operations

Employer contracts

Placement process

Communications

Support and guidance processes

Closed factories

Remploy Head Office staff

Factory employees

Unions

Media

Disability groups

General public

Future employers

PBS2

New Remploy operations

Factories decommissioned

Employee placement process

Revised internal processes

Consultation / action groups

Existing employee placements

Building disposal

...

Employer consultation process
HR contracts reviewed and revised
Media/public briefing sessions
Disability groups consultation process
Revised website & guidance materials

...

Employee consultation process

Revised process

Staff training and briefings

...

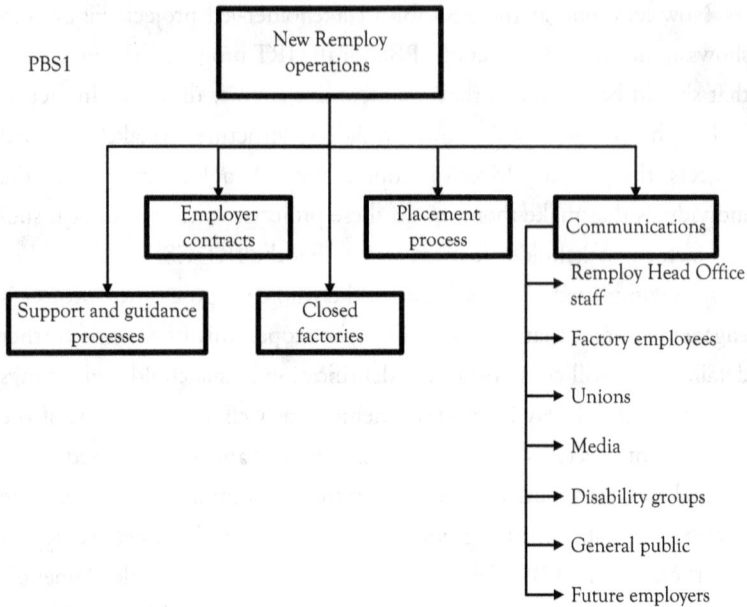

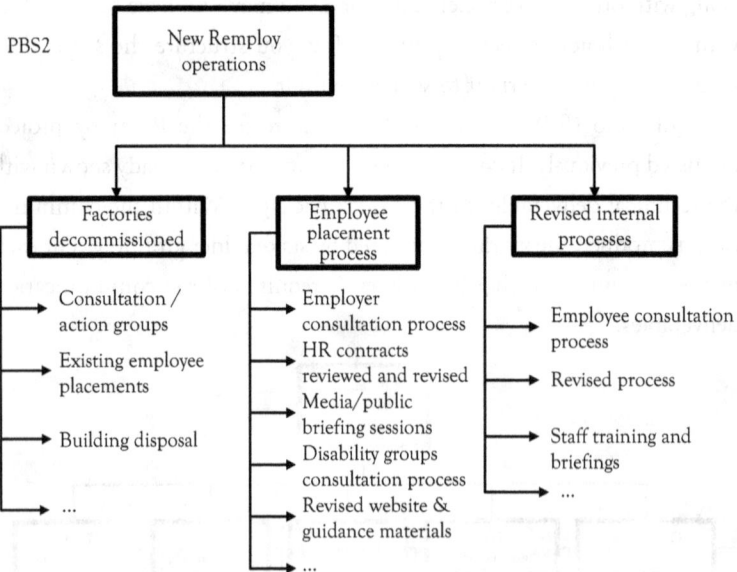

Provided for illustrative purposes only—not taken from actual plans for Remploy case

Figure 6.6 Possible alternative PBSs for Remploy

One problem with this approach is that it allows the communication and engagement elements to be seen as an 'add-on,' something that can be easily scoped out. And that's the problem—it often is!

Figure 6.6 (PBS2) identifies the principal products; decommissioned factories, the new placement processes, and internal processes and places the stakeholder engagement activities alongside the technical deliverables. Consultation with existing employees and unions is an integral part of decommissioning the factories—you can't do one without the other. PBS2 does not contain different products from PBS1, but the structuring of the project is now much more likely to focus attention and prioritize the critical stakeholder engagement outputs and activities.

The way projects are structured influences their implementation. Understanding the stakeholder mindset is critical when planning stakeholder-intensive projects like Remploy and the Cape Town IRT. The nature and level of stakeholder intensity must be reflected in the planning process—it really is too late to just add engagement on at the end.

Where did you decide to position your project on the stakeholder continuum? Is this being reflected in the planning, and delivery approaches that have been adopted? See a summary of the differences in Figure 6.7.

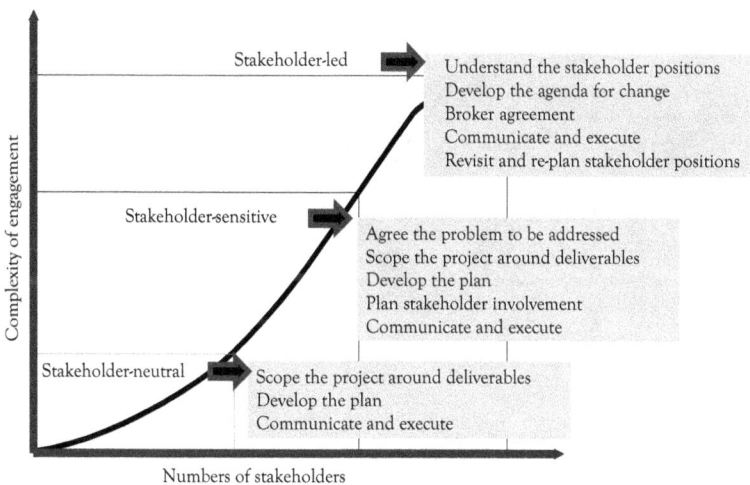

Figure 6.7 Modeling the stakeholder engagement

When Stakeholders Come First

We cannot emphasize enough, that stakeholders always matter on projects (even stakeholder-neutral ones), but in certain types of projects—stakeholder-led projects—the approach to planning and structuring projects is different. The CPPRRSS process is now dominated by the stakeholder engagement process see Figure 6.8.

The scoping of the project is best approached by scoping the stakeholder involvement, which must take place. In projects like the IRT, the agendas of powerful stakeholder groups dictate the approaches and the solutions we end up with.

In stakeholder-led projects, indirect strategies are more likely to be adopted. In the IRT case, for example, it is critical that the local transport businesses accept and commit to the new IRT; it's not just important, it's not a risk, it's a guarantee of failure if not achieved. An end-state not to be contemplated!

It is noteworthy that the project was run as a separately managed entity—a parallel project within a more extensive program. This is how you will most commonly see stakeholder-led projects executed. Parallel

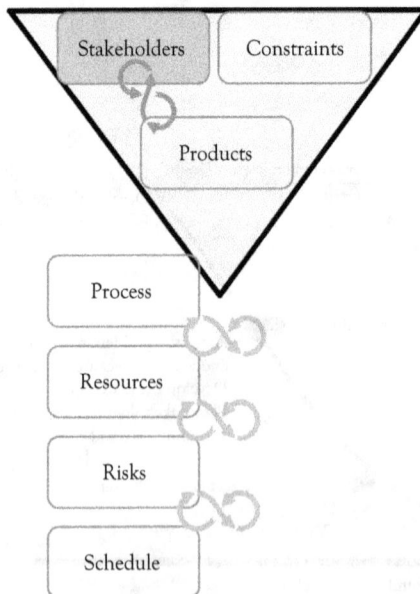

Figure 6.8 Planning steps for stakeholder-intensive projects

projects support the overall program, and while they do not specifically focus on the outputs defined in the program (in this case the rebuilding of roads and development of bus infrastructure), they do address the external stakeholder issues that arise, and that would undermine the realization of the overall program outcomes. Run as a separate but related project, stakeholder-led projects can focus on stakeholder-specific critical success factors.

Have you ever found yourself on a project where you just cannot work out what the real priorities are? Where you cannot get client agreement on the constraints or the success factors for the project? If so, then the chances are that the project either failed, had to be restructured, or at some point threatened to tear itself apart with indecision and stalling behaviors and unresolved issues. In stakeholder-led projects, the concept of the client becomes 'interesting' and complicated.

All projects exist within a hierarchy of constraints, and these ultimately dictate the structuring of every project and how decision making is made throughout the project. Constraints are owned by the client, and it is the project managers' responsibility to deliver within these. Where this is not possible, they need to help the client identify whether and how these constraints can be modified and still meet the desired outcomes.

One of the unusual and complex characteristics of planning programs is the way that the CSFs of one project can end up being managed by another project. As illustrated in the IRT program (Figure 6.9), each project had very different CSFs, and somehow or the other, these must all be achieved.

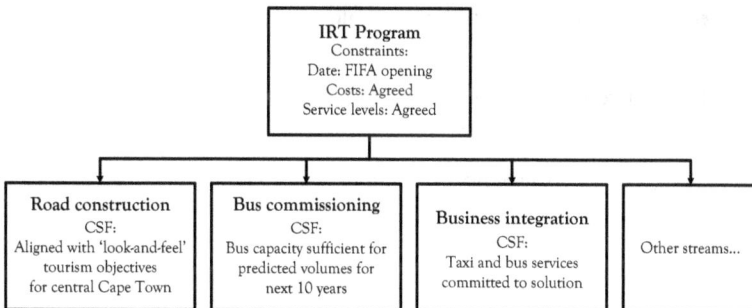

Figure 6.9 Integration of CSFs across project streams in a program

The critical success factors of a project drive the way that the project is led and managed. Putting all of the streams in Figure 6.9 together into one project would make it unmanageable. You would be unable to resolve the conflicts that result from different and competing outcomes. In programs, this is dealt with by the various planning and management disciplines, which are designed to own and manage the constraints. It is only at program level that these competing demands can be considered and evaluated and the cross-project interdependencies understood and resolved.

Reflections

All projects need stakeholder engagement. The two extremes on the stakeholder continuum (Figure 6.2) provide important learning for all projects. Stakeholder-neutral projects are dominated by role-based stakeholders and demand clear governance and a shared and committed understanding of roles and responsibilities. Stakeholder-led projects are people-complex; agendas dictate what the project can achieve and what direction it can go in. At both these extremes, the challenges are clear, if different. Consider for your projects:

1. What are the critical success factors for your project? Are they technically-focused or people-focused?
2. Which of the case studies presented in this chapter is your project most like?
3. What kind of projects do you mainly deal with? Try positioning your most recent project on the stakeholders' continuum. Was your project a stakeholder-neutral, stakeholder-sensitive, or stakeholder-led project?
4. Do you recognize any parallel projects in your business? How are they structured?
5. How have the needs of stakeholders influenced the way you plan and structure your projects?

CHAPTER 7

Planning When It Has to be Different

Projects have been around for a long time. You could argue that the Egyptian pyramid builders were involved in one. Before the 1950s, however, project management was not recognized as a distinct discipline. Between 1950 and the1980s project management came into its own. It, and particularly project planning, was seen as an exercise in a set of standard disciplined approaches, with good performance narrowly defined by compliance with a standard and a method. Since then things have changed.

Projects as Vehicles for Innovation

One of the most exciting changes is the growing involvement of project management with the delivery of innovation. It's not that innovation within projects is new. Far from it! What is becoming more prevalent is the deliberate use of projects to create and manage innovation.

Kavanagh and Naughton (2016) looked at the correlation between how a country valued project management as a discipline with the level of innovation reported by that country.

Their results (Figure 7.1) suggest that there is good evidence that the higher the project management score (measured by project qualifications taken in the country), the higher the level of innovation. Only, however, up to a point, and then the innovation score falls while the in-country project capability continues to rise.

Why would that be? The good initial correlation, followed by the separation may be a consequence of the surrogate measure used to determine project management capability. They based capability on the number of certifications gained in formal, method-based project management with its traditional approach to project planning. We believe projects are an ideal way to deliver innovation provided it is managed as an innovation project. Unless the planning, as well as other disciplines in project management, is appropriately modified, Figure 7.1 is precisely the curve we would expect.

Innovation is a slippery concept. It is clearly related to being new; sometimes it is confused with invention, and it definitely seems to imply creativity. All concepts that can, at least on the face of it, appear to be the very antithesis of the structured formalization of projects and their plans.

Fagerberg (2004) makes a helpful clarification. He argues that *Invention is the first occurrence of an idea for a new product or process, while innovation is the first attempt to carry it out into practice.* Using this idea, a project is a vehicle that transitions an invention into an innovation. This takes away the suggestion that innovation projects are responsible for creating the 'divine spark,' and leaves the sizable task as to how you structure the work of a team to allow, and even encourage out-of-the-box thinking.

Perhaps the first step is to consider a thought first mooted by Schumpeter (1961), one of the early theorists working on the management of innovation. He suggested that *All innovation is [to be] understood as a recombination of existing knowledge.* That's definitely one justification for managing innovation via projects.

Innovation vs Project management score (adapted)

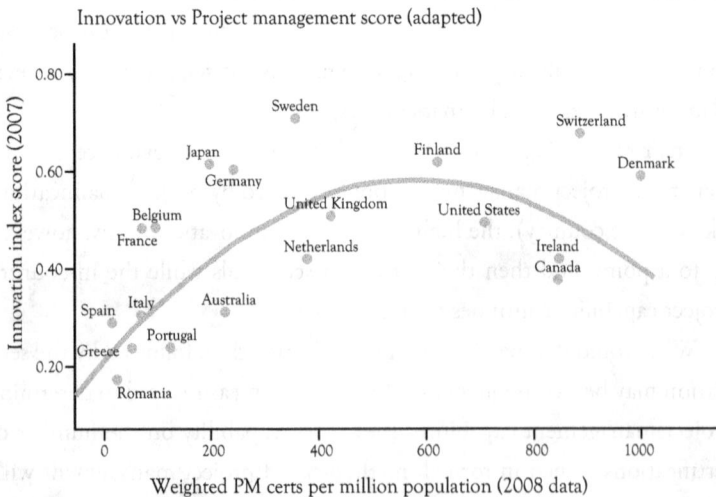

Figure 7.1 *Innovation vs. project management score*

Project teams are often a combination of specialists from various backgrounds, each with a different knowledge base. This gives rise to the need for individuals to re-examine and re-explain to other team members the basis of their viewpoint, and this encourages cross-fertilization of ideas. Now, consider the case that innovation project teams are *deliberately* made up of people with diverse backgrounds; we have the beginning of how traditional project management can and is evolving to meet this interesting challenge.

What other things should be done? We know that applying constraints in the right circumstances promotes innovation. And we also know that inappropriate application of constraints kills it. So, what is the secret formula?

Kanter (2013) set out a series of factors that she claimed were promoters of innovation. These are set out in Table 7.1. The only one that would immediately attract the eye of an experienced project manager is item 3, creating 'slack time' for resources. A phrase schedulers are familiar with, but not precisely in this context!

Table 7.1 Factors that promote innovation

1. Encourage new ideas, especially from below and from unexpected sources
2. Look ahead, not behind. The past is prologue but not necessarily precedent
3. *Leave some slack for experimentation, whether spare time or seed money*
4. Look for improvements, not critiques. Encourage collaboration toward common goals
5. Be flexible. Stress substance over form, action over the calendar. Allow for unplanned opportunities
6. Open strategic discussions to new voices
7. Accept stretch goals mean some things won't work. Avoid public humiliation; promote public recognition for innovative accomplishments
8. Foster respect for people and their talents
9. And learning is imperative. Everyone, even the most experienced, must be open to learning

Source: Kanter (2013).

The argument is that the plan (and schedule) must feature a higher tolerance for slack resources and considerably greater levels of redundancy. In this way, calendar time, effort, and thinking 'space' are created for the experimentation associated with innovation. Where traditional project managers see 'idle hands,' planners of innovation projects see opportunities for failure without penalty.

Projects and Innovation

Innovation occurs in projects. Just reflect over some of the projects that have been discussed in this book so far:

- The four-hour house—the development of superheated concrete
- The cave-rescue—a new way to hold masks on faces
- Cape Town IRT—the implementation of new retirement packages for taxi drivers
- D-Day project—new ways to compliance legal documents

> *To achieve great things two things are needed: a plan and not quite enough time.*
>
> Leonard Bernstein

You may like to consider on your projects, in what circumstances innovation has happened. In the aforementioned examples, the development of creative solutions to complex problems was driven by the constraints and occasionally the CSFs. When standard processes or products cannot achieve the desired result in the constraint set, innovation is stimulated, necessary, and welcome. On the four-house house, the development of superheating of concrete would never have occurred without the requirement to stabilize the concrete floor in such a short time. By the way, this technique was later to be used to speed up the rebuilding of highways following earthquakes in California.

For innovation to occur, the *constrained context* of the project has to be coupled with the *planned* allocation of time to seek out new solutions. Think of the cave-rescue and the practicing and sandboxing of the new mask fixing in the swimming pool before extracting comatose survivors.

There are also situations in projects where innovation is unwelcome and discouraged. Projects that do not have innovation as their purpose are supposed to have clearly defined goals. Risk-taking is deliberately managed down. Established processes are used in preference to others. Introducing unnecessary innovative solutions in a well-defined, well-constructed, and well-planned project is committing professional suicide.

This chapter is not about these kinds of projects: It's not about projects where innovation occurs because it has to, nor is it about projects where innovation happens accidentally. It is about projects whose very purpose is innovation.

Accidental Innovation

Accidental innovation occurs when the outputs and occasionally the outcomes are not quite as expected by the sponsors and key stakeholders. A surprise, but in a good way!

Two situations give rise to projects like these.

Evolutionary Projects

The first type is where a trusted process is used on a variety of ill-defined inputs. Many pharmaceutical projects are like this. Tens of thousands of tests winnow out from failed leads the possible candidates for further exploration. This, on a somewhat smaller numerical scale, is very similar to deploying Barry Boehm's (1988) spiral model used in software development projects. He recognized that it might be necessary to develop outputs evolutionarily and then preferentially develop those that look promising: *Sometimes you don't know what you want until you see it.* Evolving to a final product, where you move away from what you have, is very different from the traditional incremental model, where the design is set, and bits are added a piece at a time until complete. His spiral model (Figure 7.2) which came out of the rapid prototyping school, encapsulates the idea of 'design a little, code a little, test a little' then repeat!

Each repeated cycle is a closer approximation to some final product or to failure. At the close of each cycle, a decision is made as to whether

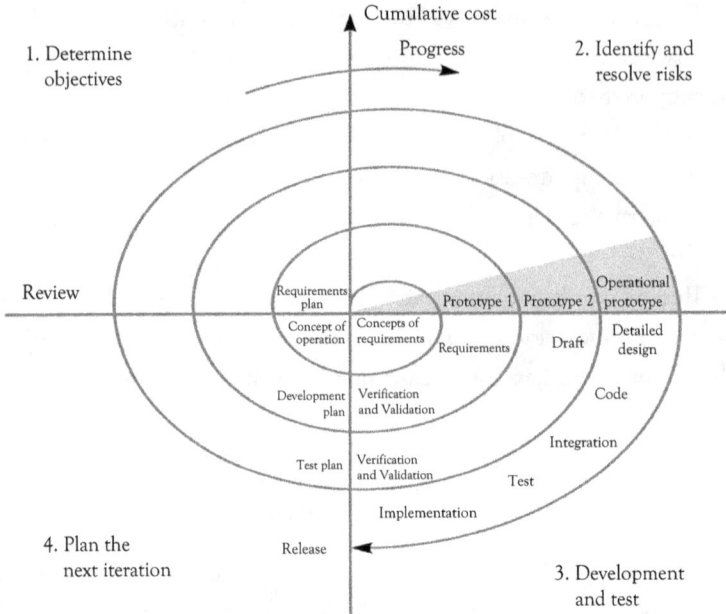

Figure 7.2 The spiral model of software development

to continue and invest more or to abandon the project. The approach is useful when the acceptance criteria (ACs)—what counts as a good solution—is unknown or poorly articulated, and the requirement givers want the opportunity to refine their needs and their wants.

The impact on the planning of these evolutionary approaches where the ACs have not been pre-established is considerable. Firstly, it is a risk-driven approach. The decision to proceed is based on the appetite for risk by the stakeholders and the degree of 'promise' in the evolving set of products. Keeping in close touch with the sponsor is also vital. Decisions to terminate a project may be based on the residual value of products, and the intelligence delivered so far.

Agile Projects

The other way accidental innovation occurs is when it is not the ACs that are poorly understood, but the problem. In these projects, the requirements are difficult to articulate, difficult to get agreement on, or are volatile.

In these circumstances, traditional planning is ineffectual and inappropriate; a fundamental piece is missing from the Project Mission Model™—what exactly is the problem?

Software development projects have been plagued over the years by poor requirements. In response, some approaches to reduce the likelihood of developing the wrong solution have been proposed. One that has a growing number of adherents is Agile, a software development framework. A particular strength of Agile, where its delivery is at its best, and traditional project management disciplines are distinctly less successful, is its use of techniques that allow requirements to *emerge*, and resources are then organized to find solutions.

There is no lack of clarity about what the ACs are that the solution must satisfy once the requirement is known. Neither is the objective vague. What can be difficult to determine in projects run using these techniques is how much of the problem will be addressed because the scope is finally determined by a time-constraint—as timeboxing is applied to the delivery of the solution.

As remarked on earlier in Chapter 2, when done well, timeboxing can be the cause of innovative solutions, but in the case of Agile this is not the primary purpose, and it would be wrong to think of Agile as an approach to manage innovation.

Intentional Innovation Projects

Keegan and Turner (2002) carried out an analysis of how innovation was being managed within projects. They concluded that (at that time) most companies were still more concerned with how to manage projects correctly, than how to manage innovation effectively. This they saw reflected in the planning processes used.

Companies that want innovation need to change what they value. Innovation projects can have loose and ambiguous goals; other projects don't. They tolerate slack resources; other projects don't, and they adopt high-risk options, use experimentation, and practice trial-and-error. Traditional projects discourage their use. To use projects to deliver innovation demands changes in planning practices and what clients and senior management expect from the planning process. This approach, and the need for project management to adapt to the need to 'fail fast, fail smart,' is highlighted by the extraordinary tale of the development of the Sidewinder air-to-air missile.

Innovation Despite Project Management?

Perhaps the single greatest modern innovation in military weapon development, certainly in terms of financial outcomes, is that of the development of the Sidewinder missile. Yet the project manager, McLean, who drove this project for 10 years, from inception to production, claims that if the project had been subjected to the project processes then required by the US Department of Defense, it could never have come to fruition. He argues that their procedures were overly bureaucratic, and particularly attacks the use of phasing and stage-gating, which, he says do not foster creativity during design. If the project had followed the standard, indeed the mandated, process, then in his mind the Sidewinder project would have been canceled in the first few years (Lenfle 2014).

The story of the development of the best-selling air-to-air missile ever built is a tale of project disciplines—end-date-based scheduling, clear sponsorship, scope management, and one-truth monitoring—all being sacrificed because the purpose of the project was to solve a problem to which no one knew the answer.

The problem was relatively simple to describe. There were two needs or requirements: a way to detect a distant very fast-moving, very maneuverable object, and a way of using that information to guide a missile to collide with the fast moving object. There was no technology available at the time that could satisfy the requirements, though the underlying science was known.

The approach adopted by the project was to set off multiple parallel design and development task forces. Successful candidates then competed in experiments run to test the performance of the prototypes. These multiple experimentations were used to refine and uncover what would ultimately be the ACs for the end product. This inverts the usual process, of shaping the solution by setting down the success criteria. As explained by McLean:

...military personnel needed a chance to test prototypes in operational situations and on the basis of this experience were in a position to write realistic requirements for the procurement of...

This runs counter to the dominant project approach used by the US Department of Defense, which demands clear and complete specifications as a necessary starting point. McLean's position, which bears more than a passing resemblance to the Agile practices of today, was that that rigid adherence to initial (and possibly wrong and undoubtedly incomplete) requirements lead to project inflexibility and failure.

Innovation Challenges for Project Management

The approach adopted by the Sidewinder project is now regarded as a good model for projects where innovation is the purpose. It emphasizes the importance of exploratory project management and the use of techniques such as 'skunkworks,' where small groups are given time and space to test out ideas, to encourage creativity by experimentation.

It suggests that when planning a project initiated to solve a problem or address an opportunity to which there is no known acceptable solution, the project should adopt a plan-do-check-act (PDCA) experimentation model. Planning is used to ensure the co-location of the team to support creative interaction and trust. It structures work into the running of experiments rather than on pre-design. It sequences work packages as independent parallel streams and encourages 'fast failure'—the rapid progression from concept to testing.

It is entirely wrong to say that in the case of innovative projects the requirements are vague or even unknown. In the case of the Sidewinder project, for example, there was no doubt what was needed, nor what the performance criteria of any proposed solution would have to meet. Innovation projects should be run when the solutions are unknown, and through *their* exploration, the understanding of the requirements evolves, which distinguishes them from projects run under evolutionary and Agile product development frameworks.

Known Problems, Unsatisfactory Solutions

Consider this example: the Navy has a requirement to be able to communicate effectively from shore to ship, from ship to ship, and from ship to ship. This need has existed for as long as there has been a navy. What has changed is what counts as acceptable solutions.

In 1840, 1920, and 1940, the Navy was content with days, minutes, and seconds as response times. Today's solutions need to provide microsecond responses to be accepted. Changes in what is regarded as acceptable and desirable in the solutions drive product and process innovation. The challenge is not in unearthing new or emergent requirements but lies in how to choose between the myriad of possible solutions.

Selection of a solution in this situation is based on using two filters. The first is the set of constraints, both physical and those arising from the projects' organizational environment. The second is the set of ACs that are derived at the time the requirements are analyzed. ACs differ from requirements as they do not belong in the problem space.

> Acceptance criteria (ACs) are the set of attributes and capabilities a solution needs to demonstrate for it to be regarded as an acceptable solution by the stakeholders.
>
> Examples of typical ACs are:
>
> 'Must be capable of turning round in less than four yards'
>
> 'The color must be pantone 67'
>
> 'The doors must be wide enough to allow a standard trailer through'
>
> Figure 7.3 shows more ACs as part of a project brief.

Take for example the first AC in the grey box. The problem is the need to reverse direction, what would count as a good solution is being able to do so in a short distance.

Constraints differ from ACs in a number of ways. We've already discussed the ownership of constraints. Most lie outside of and are independent of, the project's problem space. Their project role is to help

Ref:	Product name	Purpose
P1.1	Job profiles (JP) revised and new	To provide a view of what can expected of a person working in a specific job.

Composition (Sub products)	
One job profile per job identified. Current view is that this will include the PM defined jobs (PM1, PM2, PM3, Portfolio coordinator. Project Assistant. Programme manager. Change manager) plus two management positions	**Derivation** Based upon the PM, MSP and BCS job descriptions adapted to the client environment SAP data requirements form (as in existence in August 2012)
Side by side comparison of job profiles (the master file of job and performance characteristics)	
Underpinning competency and KPA models	
Evidence statements for proficiency levels	

Format/Presentation	
A4 job profiles in format defined by HCD processes – likely to be similar to current IS job profile descriptions in look and feel	**Conformance process** Consultation group – workshop for PM1-3 roles One on ones for PgM, Change, PfC, PjAssis positons
Excel sheet allowing side by side views and extracts of job data	IS sign-off – BC Group-wide sign off – via Portfolio programme – to be agreed

Ref:	Acceptance Criteria
JP1	The job profile will be in-line with current standards and include Job information. Quals/Exp reqts, job definition, org structure, Comms interface. KPAs. Competences and technical skills.
JP2	Sufficient distinctions between jobs exist – overlap < 30% (NB There may be similarities in technical skills but we should be able to distinguish Exp. KPAs and competences)
JP3	Domain dependent elements are separated out – a core project specialist role is identifiable.
JP4	The information requirements of the SAP system can be satisfied by the data captured in the job profile.
JP5	Career progression is supported through the use of linked competencies between jobs which may form common career routes

Ref:	Dependencies
	Talent management related initiatives:
	SAP Talent management implementation
	Leadership competences
	Implementation of changes to the job profiles will be planned around performance reviews with the PM roles being targeted for use in Oct 08

Product risks		
Description of risk	Likelihood	Impact
Cause: PM competency model not widely used	Med	High
Consequence: May be difficult to make practically usable – alternative competency models would need to be considered		

Figure 7.3 Example of a project brief with acceptance criteria

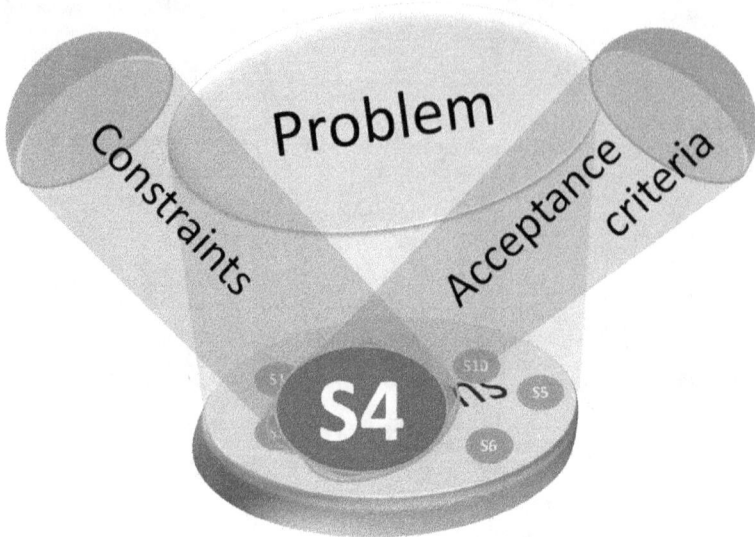

Figure 7.4 Mapping solutions to requirements

define the success criteria for the project. This tends to mean that the constraints are difficult to negotiate—sometimes their source is not even known by the project manager, or occasionally, by the project's direct governance group.

ACs, on the other hand, are local to the project. They relate directly to the problem addressed by the project. Their ownership is by groups and individuals known to the project team—and each one of the ACs is negotiable. You can see in Figure 7.4 how the impact of the constraints and ACs focus, like two spotlights, reducing the solutions under consideration to a manageable number.

Some useful outcomes emerge from the use of this model. Of immediate value is that it may indicate that there are no known solutions, given the set of constraints (including technologies), or—more commonly—no acceptable solutions given the current set of ACs. The lack of an acceptable solution is often the driver for establishing an innovation project. Another useful outcome is it suggests that the complete specification of a requirement should include its set of ACs and associated constraints.

To successfully deliver innovation the project planning processes must address the following five challenges:

The Possibility of Failure

Success in exploratory projects can be measured in part by the rate with which potential failed routes are identified and discarded, much like the test-based approach to the ZENO project discussed in Chapter 5. With failure seen as an acceptable outcome, the need is to plan for 'fail fast, fail smart'; to quickly identify when to move on to a more attractive option. Setting up processes for halting unproductive lines of inquiry is an essential part of the governance of the project. The spiral model explicitly builds these decision processes into the cycles. Agile goes one step further by not only building them in but also by keeping development cycles arbitrarily short.

Change Is Good

In innovation projects, the scope is an emergent property. The project manager and the sponsor need to be tolerant of this source of uncertainty. In these projects, planning should be seen as a frequent, even weekly, exercise, with much shorter time horizons and more reviews of the assumptions, risks, and dependencies. The logs are now as volatile as the schedule, and the need for a detailed tasking schedule is much reduced in significance. This is a natural consequence of working with knowledge workers, where positive planning is favored over procedural planning (See Worsley & Worsley (2019) for a discussion on the differences between these two types of planning.).

Taking a leaf from the Agile approach, change is not regarded as a failure; it is a signal that a new approach needs to be taken if the desired result is to be achieved. It would be wrong to interpret this propensity for change as an excuse not to plan. Planning matters in Agile projects too, because they have to give answers to questions like "What will be tackled first?" and "Can we release the test rig in April?"

A view by one of the Agile theorists who understands the need and value of plans captures the point perfectly when he comments that any plan is only one forecasted view of the future. There are others, and with the passage of time, they may be more relevant. This has to be factored into the ways planning is done, and plans are communicated.

Cohn (2005) describes planning in Agile projects as:

Planning is an attempt to find an optimal solution to the overall product development question: What should we build? To answer this question, the team considers features, resources, and schedule. The question cannot be answered all at once.

This insight is the reason for the governance difference between Agile and more traditionally conducted projects. Agile planning activity is spread across the life of the project, rather than primarily focused at the front end. That leads to the need for planning documents to be easy to amend. You should structure your plan to make the more volatile parts easier to change.

Planning should anticipate change, with change viewed as the positive consequence of having learned something and avoiding the mistake of doing something that is not wanted. As changes are discovered, plans are updated. In this sense, it follows the ideas expressed by McClean in the Sidewinder project. When managing exploratory projects, the planning is carried out, not in one go at the beginning of the project, but tranche by tranche, as positions clarify and options become available.

Maintaining Business Commitment

Without McClean, there probably would not have been a Sidewinder. There are some questionable governance issues raised in the conduct of the project. Should he have been allowed to occupy the roles of the project manager, champion, and requirements giver? Had the project not delivered such an emphatically positive result, it is likely different judgments would have been made. The idea that ultimately success is determined by history was discussed in Chapter 1. Sydney Opera House, the Scottish

Parliament Building, and a number of the railway projects would suffer from censure if judged narrowly on in-flight performance but stand as examples of outstanding human achievement today.

Exploratory projects usually don't produce results quickly. Consequently, these projects may need champions, defending the project against doubters and naysayers. Planning will need to incorporate engagement activities to promote positive branding. It may also need to stage-manage news and releases of information about progress. Interestingly, when researching high-performance projects managers, we found that one of the more highly valued skills was the ability to market their project. The process has to be done paying due deference to the sensitivities of project members. More technical project managers struggle to accept that this is a skill they need to have.

Managing Creativity

When a constraint is seen as a hindrance to achieving an objective, it can have a negative impact on productivity and creativity. If, on the other hand, a constraint is regarded as a shaper and a criterion of good performance it can have a powerfully positive effect. We have cited in this book a number of cases where this occurred. The question then is, 'How do you construct an environment in which the constraints are seen as constructive?'

Innovation projects depend on having co-workers with diverse skills and knowledge, as the diversity is the source of the innovative interactions. Motivation can be more complex in such groups, with value systems failing to coalesce. Invention may be a solo activity: individual genius unlocking new ways of thinking about things. Innovation is not. Innovation is a collaborative undertaking to socialize or monetarize a product or a process.

Techniques for forging a team for a transient endeavor are the basis of many projects. In innovation projects getting it right is a necessity and cannot be left to chance and chemistry. The planning has to include the time and the opportunity for trust and communication channels to be established. It's not a matter of everybody feeling comfortable and being liked. Team members, however, must respect their colleagues enough to feel able to challenge and to accept challenges, knowing that it is safe and expected of them.

Whether founded on fact or not, there is a scene in Apollo 13, the film, that exemplifies this point well. To integrate a newly arrived individual into a closely-knit team, the leader fabricates a situation that clearly demonstrates to the rest of the team his faith and trust in the new person. It was a deliberate ploy to develop the necessary personal commitment to each other. That's what project managers leading innovation teams need to ensure.

Funding Innovation

Perhaps of all the challenges, the hardest is the funding of innovation projects. They are not easy bedfellows with traditional projects that use some form of cost-benefit analysis. The cost-risks and the benefit-risks are in most cases not subject to any rational calculation. They have high and often indeterminate levels of uncertainty.

Those organizations that depend on innovation, including pharmaceuticals and high tech companies, have similar approaches. They almost always separate their budget for research from budgets for other investments, which includes traditional project portfolios.

In the end, it may be that the basis for providing funds for innovation will depend on a mixture of visionaries and the need to future-proof. What project management must offer is that when the money has been entrusted to its care, it will bring to bear the best techniques for translating the money into future assets that solve today's problems using tomorrow's solutions.

Reflections

The interactions between project life cycles and product development lifecycles need to be reflected in the planning approach adopted. Projects, where innovation is the purpose rather than a byproduct, are no exception.

The principal issue with planning them is the influence the governance group may exert unwittingly as it expresses its unease about lack of clarity of scope.

From your own experience, consider:

1. Have you been in situations where you had to deliberately generate opportunities for team members to learn to trust each other? How did you (or would you) go about doing that?
2. How would you plan and manage deliberately scheduled slack time? Do you think it should be structured, semi-structured, or unstructured? What is your reasoning for thinking so?
3. Have you used timeboxing to encourage innovative thinking? How did you communicate its purpose to the team? Was their reaction constructive or non-responsive?
4. Have you worked on a project with a strong champion? Was the experience positive? Are there situations where having a champion is unhelpful to the execution of a project?

CHAPTER 8

Planning Operational Projects

Many projects, and in some organizations most projects, fall into the category of operational projects. Their principle constraint is that the processes and practices of the enterprise continue without disruption.

These projects can be quite demanding. Success is often overlooked, as being noticeable probably means you are not doing it right! Stakeholders are, in the main, 'sleepers,' and only become interested when there is a problem.

A classic operational project is an office move: endless planning, little senior interest, and precious little thanks from anyone. Other common examples are projects that are 'like-for-like' replacements of technology or capability.

From Fix-on-Failure to Planned Maintenance

When you are running a set of electricity generating power plants, maintenance can be a problem. Waiting to fix-on-failure means handling unplanned outages and crisis management—always an expensive option. So the better option is to have a policy and practice of preventative maintenance, monitoring and replacing components and sub-assemblies before a problem arises. This was the approach adopted by one large energy producer. The work program had been run by line management and the process was described by one of the senior managers in a fit of frustration as "a journey into the unknown." No one knew how long it would take, or seemed to care. It took however long it took.

In 2010, a new board member decided to introduce project management disciplines into the mix. He knew that setting traditional project constraints such as time and cost was a futile exercise. The problems found could not be known at initiation, but there was one absolute constraint or success factor. As soon as the decision to take one of the turbines out of action was made, it had to be back online as soon as was practically possible. He had unwittingly set up the conditions for an operational project.

The planning steps were precise and followed the seven-step process discussed elsewhere in the book, and this time they were carried out in the sequence CPPRRSS, which is illustrated in Figure 8.1.

The set of all possible products was known, it was after all a turbine they had put in. What wasn't known was for any given product whether it needed to be left, repaired, or exchanged. So for each product, a set of processes that could be used were defined, and each process established which the resources, both human and other, set out in detail. The risks associated with the processes and resources were logged, and this complex set of alternatives was fed into a scheduling tool. As is usual with operational projects, the stakeholders were only interested in achieving an unremarkable outcome.

The change, however, was remarkable. The operational project approach with its planning provided a measure of control over the uncertainty.

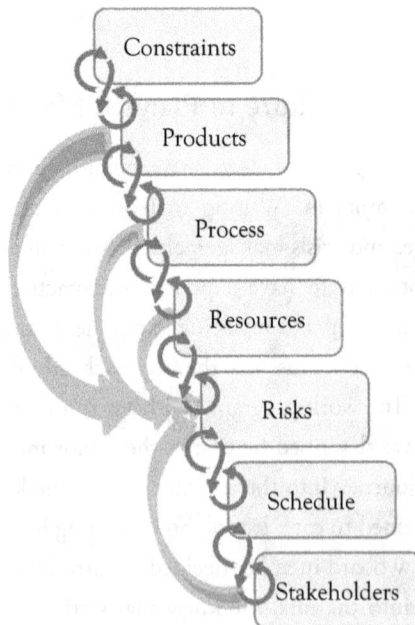

Figure 8.1 The standard CPPRRSS planning steps

Senior management felt they were once again back in the driving seat, rather than the engineers and planned outage dropped significantly.

When It Looks Like an Operational Project...But Isn't

In a similar way, a large insurance company had a policy of planned obsolescence for its IT kit. After five years, printers were replaced. This time, however, when the project was implemented, there was resistance. After a few months, whole departments flat out refused to co-operate, and the process and the project dragged on for more than two years. Why?

Although the original justification for the project was 'like-for-like' replacement and it was positioned as an operational project whose success criteria was therefore minimal disruption, it turned out there was another agenda. The Head of IT and the owner of the printer assets had her own critical success factor. She wanted to reduce costs—a genuine benefit—which is unusual for most operational projects. She also wanted to implement what to her was an important improvement—the direct allocation of printer costs as opposed to the arbitrary allocation of costs that then prevailed. Chaos, anger, and resentment! When you run operational projects, and many, many projects are operational projects, it is essential the game plan is understood. None of the planning and few of the project disciplines that flow from setting projects up as operational will support the management of significant impacts on stakeholders' behaviors.

When Is a Project a Project?

While there are many operational projects, there are also a lot of miscreants—pieces of work masquerading as projects—that are creating havoc. Let's consider these four common situations:

1. A 'project' that is, in fact, a continuing series of process improvement activities.
2. A 'project' that is a piece of work carried by just one person.
3. A 'project' that is a standard process executed regularly, for example, creating an annual report.
4. A 'project' set up to maintain existing equipment or systems and is:

(a) Carried out to prevent a problem arising (preventative maintenance).

(b) Carried out to fix a problem that has arisen (corrective maintenance).

(c) Done to improve performance (perfective maintenance)—also called 'enhancement.'

All of these types of activities are called projects and are found in project portfolios in many organizations. They are also the source of considerable distress in these organizations as managers and members of the project community struggle with the clash between the diktat of method enforced by a control-oriented project office and commonsense.

Yes, you can show that each activity does have some management aspects in common with a project, but they really aren't projects, and a major disservice is done by mistakenly calling them so. Let's revisit the definition of a project and the purpose of planning in projects:

A project is a temporary organization set up to manage the inherent uncertainty caused when resources are assigned to undertake a unique and transient endeavor within a set of constraints and needs to integrate the outputs created into a changed future state that delivers beneficial outcomes. And the purpose of planning in projects is to manage those sources of uncertainty.

When you try to apply this definition to the four situations, it becomes clear that they fail on many counts. They are not temporary organizations of individuals. They have not been brought together for a unique and transient process. The constraints are usually not enforced or enforceable. And finally, and crucially, there are virtually no sources of significant uncertainty, the people doing the work are familiar users of standard processes, the solution sought is known—and no one is interested in the problem space, the requirement is to deliver the known solution.

It is worth looking in more detail at (4) *maintain existing equipment or systems.* When preventative maintenance is implemented as a continuous improvement program, it gains no benefit from being set up as any type of project. Corrective maintenance activities are inherently unplannable. They are transactional events that demand immediate reaction or the response can be batched with others and deferred. There are no project-like aspects in this type of work. The third type, perfective maintenance, also referred to as enhancement projects, can benefit from being dealt with as a project, but the use of project disciplines is often rightly abbreviated.

So why does it matter if these pieces of work are called and treated like projects? What's in a name? Well, quite a bit!

Confusing Work Package Management with Project Management

At best these pieces of work are what we call 'work packages.' They are distinguishable from projects because, if work packages can have an objective, then the objective is to deliver the product, not a future state. The conditions of success are that the product is delivered as near defect-free as maybe, and if there is a stakeholder, then they will be the product owner. The planning, if there is any, can be wholly defined by PPS, which translates to: establish the *products;* set out the *processes;* define the *schedule.* The resources are preset, the risks are generic, and in truth, most of the processes are pre-determined. The dominant life cycle is not the project life cycle with its start, plan, do, close structure, but a *product life cycle,* be it a document, engineering, or an IT product development model, such as waterfall or Agile.

This gives rise to two concerns. The first is that using project disciplines in inappropriate circumstances leads either to their disuse or their misuse when it matters. You don't need to be doing corrective maintenance long before you realize that planning, scheduling and the maintenance of risk logs, let alone other project disciplines, is just 'make work.' You just need to get on with it—it's a lot like process management! With this lesson well learned, it gets carried over to situations where planning and structuring work using project disciplines actually does matter, but it does not get done. This may well be why planning in projects is so poorly done if done at all. The training ground of many project managers is in the management of work packages, flaunted as projects.

The other concern is that it reinforces in managers and senior managers' minds that planning, and other documentation, is bureaucracy, a misuse of time and effort.

By managing work packages as projects, the organization either gets involved in over-governance—you do not need a sponsor or a steering group for these activities—or worse, neglect the governance of projects.

By putting work packages with projects in a single project portfolio, the organization generates, often overwhelming, competition for resources, with these urgent but relatively unimportant bits of work displacing projects with genuine benefit cases, or else creating an ever-growing backlog of items not done, to the frustration of many.

By conflating work packages with projects it legitimizes the inappropriate extension of product life cycles into project management, and history proves this is pernicious. In the 1970s, there was a surge of IT technicians into project management, which damaged and delayed the development of project management by 20 years or more. You can still see the fossil remains in many organizations today when you look at their project life cycles.

There was a product development life cycle called SSADM, which stood for structured systems analysis and design method. Heralded as a breakthrough—and it was—in formalizing and in many ways simplifying the process of creating complex software, it provided the basis for the evolution of systems engineering approaches. What became a problem was the unnatural, unwelcome, and inappropriate extension of its concepts and approach into project management.

SSADM urged that analysis comes first—a really good idea! Then design, build, and test followed by implementation. This is a sensible and organized way to produce complex products and a hopelessly incomplete—and unhelpful—way to manage a project. Yet in many organizations, even today, you can recognize SSADM stages featured in their customized and carefully crafted *project* life cycle. It's no wonder when projects are run under these circumstances that they ignore stakeholders, omit closedown, forget about benefits and change! Of course, they do. Product life cycles have nothing to say about them. We could do well to heed the lesson and make sure we don't repeat the experience as Agilists push their product development life cycle as a candidate for running projects.

The Special Concerns of Operational Projects

Operational projects are so prevalent in organizations that it is worth taking a moment to understand some of the dynamics and how they differ from other projects discussed in this book.

Operational projects are often staffed either in whole or in part by operational personnel. In fact, the individuals running these projects may not identify themselves with or as project managers. They do, and want to, use many of the project disciplines, but shy away from what they see as the bureaucracy of project method.

One distinctive aspect is how quickly these projects can slide from managed scheduled activities—where work done is organized by tasks and milestones—to become a 'best endeavors' piece of work. 'Best endeavors' means that the work will get done when it gets done—not a well-publicized project ambition! The problem is that the *urgencies* of operational imperatives trump what may well be the more *important* work of the project. And, this is exacerbated further when the project team members are also operational staff. The conflict gives rise to the observation, that for operational projects, the only genuinely hard constraint is minimum disruption, not, despite all claims to the contrary, costs, deadlines, or anything else.

Abraham Lincoln is said to have commented that if he had six hours to cut down a tree, he would spend the first four hours sharpening the axe. Just as well he was a president then because the widespread use of operational projects leads to the apparently irrational situation of the organization being too busy to improve its performance.

Reflections

Operational projects are the commonest type of project, and project-like activity encountered, with some organizations having more than 80 percent of their resources committed to them.

Consider these questions in light of your own experiences:

1. How do small enhancement types of projects get started? Does your organization use any of the Agile-inspired approaches such as Kanban or tools such as Jira to prioritize take-on? Would they help?

2. For the vast majority of operational projects there is little or no need to establish their strategic aspects, so using the Project Mission Model™ is unnecessary. There are, however, risks in not using it, what do you think they might be?

3. We argue that many 'operational projects' should be treated as work packages as they do not benefit from the use of project management disciplines. What is your experience, and what is your view on this?

4. Has your organization used Agile approaches for the development of software? What do you think about the debate about Agile-based project management?

5. In many operational projects, the resources available for use on the project are predetermined. How would you handle this in the CPPRRSS model?

CHAPTER 9

And Finally…

The tour of project planning, and how it varies depending on the project's context is complete. There are just a few points we would like to share.

It turns out that project managers do have a natural preference for one approach to project management over the others—and this varies from project manager to project manager. When there is a good match between the project type and project manager, then things are easier. If the match is poor—problems! Given this, naturally, the next question is: Is there such a thing as a professional project manager? Can you develop project managers to manage appropriately, irrespective of the type of project they find themselves managing? The short answer is that you can. Not everyone, and sometimes not easily, because it is about attitudes as well as knowledge and skill, but it can be done. It goes a long way beyond knowledge of a method.

What seems to be a distinguishing characteristic of high-performance project managers is that they recognize and adapt their approach to planning and execution of projects in line with the different challenges. The planning approach varies as we have discussed and the plans created are not interchangeable between projects. If the conditions of success for a project changes, the project needs to be re-planned.

The different conditions of success for these types of projects affect the way that CPPRRSS model is used. The differences are summarized in Figure 9.1.

We leave you then with two final thoughts. Project management, despite its checkered history of success, is the most influential management approach of the twentieth century, and many great things have been done using it. Gaining mastery over uncertainty by using plans to shape the world; structuring the work people do and ordering the environment to make things possible, gives a great sense of accomplishment and is a wonderful feeling. We suggest you go and enjoy it.

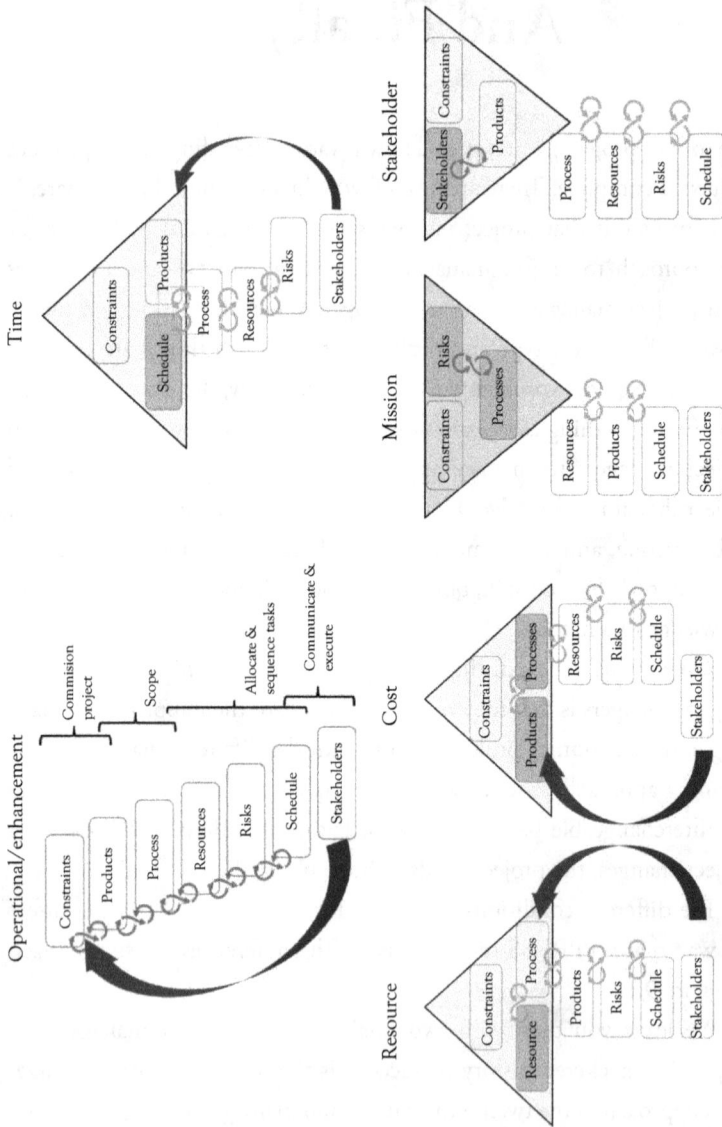

Figure 9.1 Planning approach based on constraint type

References

Boehm, B.W. 1981. *Software Engineering Economics*, 197 vols. Englewood Cliffs, NJ: Prentice-hall.

Brooks, F.P., Jr. 1995. *The Mythical Man-Month: Essays on Software Engineering.* Anniversary Edition, 2/E. Pearson Education India.

Change Diamond™ is a Registered Trademark of CITI Limited.

Churchill, N.C. 1984. "Budget Choice-Planning vs. Control." *Harvard Business Review* 62, no. 4, p. 150.

Cohn, M. 2005. *Agile Estimating and Planning*. Pearson Education.

Fagerberg, J. 2004. *Innovation: A Guide to the Literature*. Georgia Institute of Technology.

Flyvbjerg, B., N. Bruzelius, and W. Rothengatter. 2003. *Megaprojects and Risk: An Anatomy of Ambition*. Cambridge University Press.

Four Corners. 2018. "Divers Reveal Extraordinary Behind-the-Scenes Details of Thailand cave rescue." Available at https://youtu.be/-esjQLvsgTs (accessed August 06, 2018).

Gilb, T., and S. Finzi. 1988. *Principles of Software Engineering Management*, 11 vols. Reading, MA: Addison-Wesley.

Goldratt, E.M., and J. Cox. 1984. *The Goal, Croton-on-Hudson*. New York, NY: North River Press Inc.

Goldratt, E.M. 1997. *Critical Chain*. Great Barrington, MA: North River Press.

Kanter, R.M. 2013. "Nine Rules for Stifling Innovation." *Harvard Business Review* [Online], available at https://hbr.org/2013/01/nine-rules-for-stifling-innova (accessed August 09, 2018).

Kavanagh, D., and E. Naughton. 2016. *Innovation and Project Management-Exploring the Inks*, 2nd ed. PM World Journal, Volume V, Issue II, February.

Lenfle, S. 2014. "Toward a Genealogy of Project Management: Sidewinder and the Management of Exploratory Projects." *International Journal of Project Management* 32, no. 6, pp. 921–31.

Leonard, D., and L. Willis. 2000. "Is Project Manager Capability Domain Specific?" *Congress 2000 Proceedings*, IPMA.

McConnell, S. 2006. *Software Estimation: Demystifying the Black Art*. Microsoft press.

Meng, X., and B. Gallagher. 2012. "The Impact of Incentive Mechanisms on Project Performance." *International Journal of Project Management* 30, no. 3, pp. 352–62.

PRINCE2® is a Registered Trademark of AXELOS.

Project Management Institute (PMI). 2013. *A Guide to the Project Management Body of Knowledge* (PMBOK® Guide), 5th ed. Newtown Square, PA: Author.

Project Mission Model™ is a Registered Trademark of CITI Limited.

Schumpeter, J.A. 1961. *The Theory of Economic Development: An Inquiry into Profits, Capital, Credit, Interest, and the Business Cycle* (1912/1934). Google Scholar.

Shenhar, A.J., O. Levy, and D. Dvir. 1997. "Mapping the Dimensions of Project Success." *Project Management Journal* 28, no. 2, pp. 5–13.

Turner, J.R. 1999. *Gower Handbook of Project Management*, 4th ed. Aldershot, UK: Gower Publishing.

Turner, J.R., and R. Müller. 2003. "On the Nature of the Project as a Temporary Organization." *International Journal of Project Management* 21, no. 1, pp. 1–8.

Turner, J.R. 2014. *Handbook of Project-Based Management*, 92 vols. New York, NY: McGraw-hill.

Worsley, L.M. 2009. "The Characteristics of Successful Project Managers: Insights from Across Sector Profiling of Project Managers." *Modernisation in Project Management*, pp. 1–9.

Worsley, L.M. 2010. "Remploy–A Case of Super-Sensitive, Stakeholder Management." *The Project Manager*, 6 (accessed September 2010).

Worsley, L.M. 2016. *Stakeholder-Led Project Management: Changing the Way We Manage Projects*. Business Expert Press.

Worsley, L.M., and C.J. Worsley. 2019. *The Lost Art of Planning Projects*. Business Expert Press. http://pmknowledgecenter.com/dynamic_scheduling/risk/critical-chainbuffer-management-adding-buffers-project-schedule (accessed August 16, 2018).

About the Authors

Louise Worsley has been a project management consultant, lecturer, and coach for nearly thirty years. She is a visiting lecturer at the University of Cape Town on the MSc in Project Management.

Louise is a regular contributor to project management online forums, a judge in the Global Alliance PMO Awards, joint leader of the Success Stories Shared PMSA initiative to encourage the sharing of experiences and learning across the project manager community, and author of "Stakeholder-led Management: Changing the way we manage projects" (Worsley 2016).

Christopher Worsley has been the CEO of CITI Limited since 1991. CITI is a UK-based company dedicated to developing organizational and personal capabilities in project and program management within corporate organizations and government. He has been involved in the development of project and program management as practiced in the UK for over 45 years, including the launch of PRINCE2® and some PM accreditations.

Christopher has worked on over 150 transformation programs—either as the program manager or program architect, or as a lead assessor on program assurance teams. He is a senior advisor on project and program performance to a number of large corporations in South Africa and the UK.

About the Authors

Index

OTHER TITLES IN OUR PORTFOLIO AND PROJECT MANAGEMENT COLLECTION

Timothy J. Kloppenborg, Editor

- *Project Portfolio Management: A Model for Improved Decision Making* by Clive N. Enoch
- *Project Management Essentials* by Kathryn Wells and Timothy J. Kloppenborg
- *The Agile Edge: Managing Projects Effectively Using Agile Scrum* by Brian Vanderjack
- *Project Teams: A Structured Development Approach* by Vittal S. Anantatmula
- *Attributes of Project-Friendly Enterprises* by Vittal S. Anantatmula and Parviz F. Rad
- *Stakeholder-led Project Management: Changing the Way We Manage Projects* by Louise M. Worsley
- *Innovative Business Projects: Breaking Complexities, Building Performance, Volume One: Fundamentals and Project Environment* by Rajagopal
- *Innovative Business Projects: Breaking Complexities, Building Performance, Volume Two: Financials, New Insights, and Project Sustainability* by Rajagopal
- *Why Projects Fail: Nine Laws for Success* by Tony Martyr
- *Project-Based Learning: How to Approach, Report, Present, and Learn from Course-Long Projects* by Harm-Jan Steenhuis and Lawrence Rowland

Announcing the Business Expert Press Digital Library

Concise e-books business students need for classroom and research

This book can also be purchased in an e-book collection by your library as

- a one-time purchase,
- that is owned forever,
- allows for simultaneous readers,
- has no restrictions on printing, and
- can be downloaded as PDFs from within the library community.

Our digital library collections are a great solution to beat the rising cost of textbooks. E-books can be loaded into their course management systems or onto students' e-book readers.
The **Business Expert Press** digital libraries are very affordable, with no obligation to buy in future years. For more information, please visit **www.businessexpertpress.com/librarians**. To set up a trial in the United States, please email **sales@businessexpertpress.com**.

www.ingramcontent.com/pod-product-compliance
Lightning Source LLC
Chambersburg PA
CBHW061317220326
41599CB00026B/4924